CAKES

CAKES

MORE THAN 140 DELECTABLE BAKES FOR TEA TIME, DESSERTS,
PARTIES AND EVERY SPECIAL OCCASION

Ann Nicol

LORENZ BOOKS

This edition is published by Lorenz Books, an imprint of Anness Publishing Ltd, 108 Great Russell Street, London WC1B 3NA; info@anness.com

www.lorenzbooks.com;
www.annesspublishing.com

If you like the images in this book and would like to investigate using them for publishing, promotions or advertising, please visit our website www.practicalpictures.com for more information.

Publisher: Joanna Lorenz
Editor: Anne Hildyard
Designer: Nigel Partridge
Production Controller: Ben Worley
Photographers: William Lingwood and
    Nicki Dowey

PUBLISHER'S NOTE
Although the advice and information in this book are believed to be accurate and true at the time of going to press, neither the authors nor the publisher can accept any legal responsibility or liability for any errors or omissions that may have been made nor for any inaccuracies nor for any loss, harm or injury that comes about from following instructions or advice in this book.

NOTES
Bracketed terms are intended for American readers.
For all recipes, quantities are given in both metric and imperial measures and, where appropriate, in standard cups and spoons. Follow one set of measures, but not a mixture, because they are not interchangeable.
Standard spoon and cup measures are level. 1 tsp = 5ml, 1 tbsp = 15ml, 1 cup = 250ml/8fl oz.
Australian standard tablespoons are 20ml. Australian readers should use 3 tsp in place of 1 tbsp for measuring small quantities.
American pints are 16fl oz/2 cups. American readers should use 20fl oz/2.5 cups in place of 1 pint when measuring liquids.
Electric oven temperatures in this book are for conventional ovens. When using a fan oven, the temperature will probably need to be reduced by about 10–20°C/20–40°F. Since ovens vary, you should check with your manufacturer's instruction book for guidance.
The nutritional analysis given for each recipe is calculated per portion (i.e. serving or item), unless otherwise stated. If the recipe gives a range, such as Serves 4–6, then the nutritional analysis will be for the smaller portion size, i.e. 6 servings. The analysis does not include optional ingredients, such as salt added to taste.
Medium (US large) eggs are used unless otherwise stated.
Main image on front cover shows *Chocolate and Beetroot Layer Cake*. For the recipe, see page 92.

Contents

Introduction

With its mix of easy recipes and more challenging cakes, this volume is ideal for both beginners and experienced bakers. It has a perfect blend of all the familiar, classic cakes as well as including more modern, innovative ideas to inspire you.

CAKES FOR ALL OCCASIONS

There is always a good reason for baking a cake: it could be a birthday, wedding, anniversary or some other celebration. A beautiful cake is often the highlight or climax of a party, with candles to blow out or a wonderfully decorated cake to cut.

This volume provides something for everyone, whether it is a custom-made cake for a special occasion or just an everyday tea-time treat such as a light sponge, loaf cake, teabread or tray bake.

Each chapter deals with a different type of cake, from traditional cakes through fruit cakes, spice, nut and seed cakes, dessert cakes and cheesecakes, chocolate cakes and special occasion cakes to a wide selection of little cakes that are fun to make and so appealing to look at.

STARTING TO BAKE

Cake making is a matter of getting the right ingredients, good-quality equipment and then systematically following a tried-and-tested method.

There are several elements that can affect the finished result: weighing the exact amount of ingredients, the correct oven temperature, and cooking the cake for the right time. Testing that your cake is fully cooked becomes second nature after a while, but can make the difference to the final result.

CAKE SELECTION

The recipes included in this book are aimed at different skill levels, some may look intricate, yet they are quick and easy to make. Others require a little more experience.

Classic sponge cakes includes all the well known cake recipes that you will use again and again, such as Madeira Cake, Boston Cream Pie, Carrot Cake with Cream Cheese Frosting and Victoria Sponge. All kinds of variations appear in the chapter on Fruit cakes: as well as classic Dundee Cake and Rich Fruit Cake, there are lighter versions with fresh rather than dried fruit, including Streusel-Topped Peach Cake and Crunchy-topped Fresh Apricot Cake, which can also be eaten warm as a dessert, served with cream or natural (plain) yogurt. Adding raisins, sultanas (golden raisins), dates

LEFT: *Made with apricots, pecan nuts and white chocolate, White Chocolate Blondies are the perfect treat at any time of the day.*

ABOVE: *Mini Victoria Sponge Pops are sure to be as popular as the larger version.*

ABOVE: *Chocolate Drizzle Party Cake is a stunning cake to celebrate any occasion.*

ABOVE: *This sumptuous cake is a fat-free, Fresh Fruit Genoese Sponge.*

and apricots to cakes ensures they are moist and the fruits contain vitamins and minerals as well as fibre.

Spice, nut and seed cakes such as Apple and Cinnamon Cake or Yogurt Cake with Pistachio Nuts use every type of nut and spice, adding crunchy texture and flavour.

Chocolate cakes will always be happily received, and there are many irresistible versions here. Death by Chocolate, Devil's Food Cake, Black Forest Gateau, Mississippi Mud Cake and Sachertorte are just a few of the traditional cakes; more inventive cakes on offer are Chocolate and Beetroot Layer Cake and Chocolate Potato Cake.

Two of the versatile dessert cake recipes are creamy baked Rum and Raisin Cheesecake and Chocolate Brandy-snap Gateau.

In the next section, some of the Special Occasion Cakes are made ahead or in stages. Although they look professional, many are achievable, and some, such as Easy Birthday Cake, are very simple to make. Mother's Day Cake or Rose-petal Wedding Cake are perfect for family occasions.

For everyday baking for tea time, coffee mornings, fêtes, bazaars and picnics, loaf cakes and tray bakes are ideal. They can be made ahead and stored in airtight containers or frozen undecorated. Sticky Toffee Traybake,

Vanilla Streusel Bars and Banana Bread are just a small selection of the appealing recipes in this chapter.

Finally, the section of little cakes includes Rich Chocolate Ruffles and Spangled Sugar Cupcakes, which are perfect for parties. Some of the new, fun cakes are Mango Passion Whoopie Pies, Red Velvet Pops, Black Forest Pops and Glorious Wedding Day Pops.

USING THIS BOOK
At the end of the book is a section outlining the basic preparation, ingredients, bakeware and other equipment, methods of making cakes, and recipes for fillings, frostings and toppings, and how to use them.

Classic Sponge Cakes

For the perfect treat with a cup of tea or coffee, there is nothing like an airy sponge cake filled with cream, fruit or jam, and frosted with a light, fluffy icing. This section contains the most popular, traditional cakes, including Victoria Sponge, Boston Cream Pie, and Frosted Walnut Layer Cake. There are recipes for all levels of skills: for example, Carrot Cake with Cream Cheese Icing looks very appealing but is simple to make.

Easy all-in-one sponge

This strawberry and 'cream' cake is so quick and easy to make. Store for up to three days in an airtight container, or freeze, undecorated, for up to two months.

SERVES 12

175g/6oz/1½ cups self-raising
    (self-rising) flour
5ml/1 tsp baking powder
175g/6oz/¾ cup soft tub margarine,
    plus extra for greasing
175g/6oz/scant 1 cup caster
    (superfine) sugar
3 eggs
15ml/1 tbsp milk
5ml/1 tsp vanilla extract

FOR THE FILLING AND TOPPING
150g/5oz white chocolate chips
200g/7oz/scant 1 cup cream cheese
25g/1oz/¼ cup icing
    (confectioners') sugar
30ml/2 tbsp strawberry jam
12 strawberries

1 Preheat the oven to 180°C/350°F/ Gas 4. Grease and line two 20cm/8in round shallow cake tins (pans) with baking parchment.

2 Sift the flour and baking powder into a bowl, then add the remaining cake ingredients. Beat until smooth, then divide between the tins.

3 Bake for 20 minutes. Leave to stand for 5 minutes, then turn out on to a wire rack to cool. Remove the lining papers.

4 To make the filling and topping, melt the chocolate chips in a heatproof bowl over a pan of gently simmering water. Remove from the heat and cool slightly, then beat in the cream cheese and icing sugar.

5 Spread the top of one sponge with jam. Slice 4 strawberries, then arrange them over the jam.

6 Spread one-third of the filling over the base of the other cake.

7 Put the cakes together. Spread the remaining topping over the cake top. Decorate with strawberries.

Nutritional information per portion: Energy 395kcal/ 1648kJ; Protein 4.7g; Carbohydrate 39.6g, of which sugars 28.5g; Fat 25.3g, of which saturates 15.2g; Cholesterol 94mg; Calcium 90mg; Fibre 0.5g; Sodium 173mg.

Almond and raspberry-filled roll

This light and airy whisked sponge cake is rolled up with a filling of raspberries and cream. It is also good with other soft fruits, such as small or sliced strawberries, or blackcurrants. Eat fresh.

SERVES 8

butter, for greasing
4 eggs
115g/4oz/generous ½ cup caster
    (superfine) sugar, plus extra
    for dusting
150g/5oz/1¼ cups plain (all-purpose)
    flour, sifted
25g/1oz/¼ cup ground almonds

FOR THE FILLING

250ml/8fl oz/1 cup double
    (heavy) cream
275g/10oz/1⅔ cups fresh raspberries
toasted flaked (sliced) almonds,
    to decorate

1 Preheat the oven to 200°C/400°F/ Gas 6. Grease and line a 33 × 23cm/ 13 × 9in Swiss roll tin (jelly roll pan) with baking parchment.

2 Put the eggs and sugar in a large bowl and beat with an electric whisk for about 10 minutes, or until the mixture is thick and pale.

3 Sift the flour over the mixture and gently fold in with the ground almonds, using a metal spoon.

4 Spoon the batter into the tin and smooth the top level with a spoon. Bake for 10–12 minutes, or until the sponge is well risen and springy to the touch.

5 Dust a sheet of baking parchment liberally with caster sugar. Turn out the cake on to the paper, and cool with the tin still in place. Remove the tin and peel off the lining paper.

6 To make the filling, whip the cream until it holds its shape. Fold in 250g/8oz/1¼ cups of the raspberries, and spread over the cooled cake, leaving a border.

7 Carefully roll up the cake from a narrow end, using the paper to lift the sponge.

8 Dust with caster sugar. Serve the roll decorated with the remaining raspberries and the toasted flaked almonds.

Nutritional information per portion: Energy 271kcal/ 1127kJ; Protein 4.7g; Carbohydrate 16.7g, of which sugars 11.9g; Fat 21.1g, of which saturates 11.2g; Cholesterol 114mg; Calcium 56mg; Fibre 1.2g; Sodium 35mg.

Fresh fruit Genoese sponge

Genoese is the original fatless sponge, which can be used for luxury gateaux and Swiss rolls. It has a soft and light texture, but as it is made without fat it should be eaten soon after making.

SERVES 8–10

butter, for greasing
4 eggs
115g/4oz/generous ½ cup caster
   (superfine) sugar
175g/6oz/1½ cups plain (all-purpose)
   flour, sifted

FOR THE FILLING AND TOPPING
90ml/6 tbsp orange-flavoured liqueur such
   as Cointreau

600ml/1 pint/2½ cups double
   (heavy) cream
60ml/4 tbsp vanilla sugar
450g/1lb/4 cups fresh soft fruit, such as
   raspberries, strawberries, redcurrants
   and blueberries
65g/2½oz/½ cup shelled pistachio nuts,
   finely chopped
60ml/4 tbsp apricot jam, warmed and
   sieved (strained), optional

1 Preheat the oven to 180°C/350°F/Gas 4. Grease and line a 21cm/8½in round deep cake tin (pan) with baking parchment.

2 Beat the eggs and sugar in a bowl with an electric whisk for 10 minutes, or until the mixture is thick and pale. Sift the pre-sifted flour into the bowl with the egg and sugar mixture, then fold together gently.

3 Transfer the batter to the prepared tin. Bake in the centre of the oven for 30–35 minutes, or until a skewer inserted into the centre of the cake comes out clean. Leave for 5 minutes, then turn out on to a wire rack to cool. Peel off the lining paper.

4 Cut the cake in half horizontally. Put the bottom layer on to a serving plate. Sprinkle the orange-flavoured liqueur, if using, over the cut side of each cake. To make the filling and topping, put the cream and vanilla sugar in a bowl and beat with an electric whisk until the mixture holds its shape.

5 Spread two-thirds of the cream over the bottom layer of the cake and add half of the soft fruit. Top with the second layer and spread the remaining cream over the top. Arrange the rest of the fruit on the top and sprinkle with the pistachio nuts.

6 If you like, lightly glaze the top layer of fruit by brushing over the warmed apricot jam.

Nutritional information per portion: Energy 815kcal/3411kJ; Protein 8.5g; Carbohydrate 99.6g, of which sugars 85.9g; Fat 43g, of which saturates 21.8g; Cholesterol 158mg; Calcium 128mg; Fibre 2g; Sodium 132mg.

Victoria sponge

This light cake was named in honour of Queen Victoria of England. Often referred to as a Victoria sandwich, the mixture is based on equal quantities of fat, sugar and flour. It is usually pressed together with a layer of jam. Store this cake for up to three days in an airtight container.

SERVES 6–8

175g/6oz/¾ cup butter, softened, plus extra for greasing
3 large eggs
a few drops of vanilla extract
175g/6oz/scant 1 cup caster (superfine) sugar
175g/6oz/1½ cups self-raising (self-rising) flour
about 60ml/4 tbsp jam
icing (confectioners') sugar, for dusting

1 Preheat the oven to 180°C/350°F/Gas 4. Grease and line two 20cm/8in round shallow cake tins (pans) with baking parchment.

2 In a small bowl, lightly beat the eggs with the vanilla extract.

3 In a large bowl, beat the butter with the sugar until the mixture is pale, light and fluffy, then beat in the eggs in small quantities, beating well after each addition.

4 Sift the flour over the top in two batches and, using a metal spoon, fold in lightly using a figure-of-eight motion until the mixture is smooth.

5 Divide the batter between the prepared tins and smooth out to the edges so that the mixture is level. Bake for 20 minutes, or until golden and firm to the touch in the centre of the cake.

6 Leave the cakes to cool in the tins for a few minutes, then turn out on to a wire rack to go cold. Remove the lining paper.

7 Spread one cake with jam and sandwich the layers together.

8 Sift a little icing sugar over the top before serving.

Nutritional information per portion: Energy 368kcal/1543kJ; Protein 4.6g; Carbohydrate 44.7g, of which sugars 28.5g; Fat 20.3g, of which saturates 12g; Cholesterol 118mg; Calcium 104mg; Fibre 0.7g; Sodium 241mg.

Pound cake

The original pound cake, enjoyed both in the USA and Britain for many years, was made using 450g/1lb of each ingredient with as many as eight eggs to raise it. This recipe is for a smaller variation and is served warm with a delicious, fresh fruit sauce. Keep for up to three days.

SERVES 6–8

175g/6oz/³⁄₄ cup butter, softened, plus
  extra for greasing
175g/6oz/³⁄₄ cup caster (superfine)
  sugar, plus extra for sprinkling
175g/6oz/1¹⁄₂ cups plain
  (all-purpose) flour
10ml/2 tsp baking powder
3 eggs
grated rind of 1 orange
15ml/1 tbsp orange juice

FOR THE SAUCE

450g/1lb/4 cups fresh raspberries
  or strawberries
25g/1oz/2 tbsp caster
  (superfine) sugar
15ml/1 tbsp lemon juice

1 To make the sauce, reserve a few fruits for decoration. Process the remaining fruit until smooth in a food processor.

2 Add the sugar and lemon juice, and process to combine. Strain and chill the sauce.

3 Preheat the oven to 180°C/350°F/ Gas 4. Grease a 20cm/8in round ring tin (pan). Sprinkle the base and sides lightly with sugar.

4 Sift the flour with the baking powder into a bowl.

5 In another bowl, beat the butter until creamy. Add the remaining sugar and beat until light and fluffy. Add the eggs, one at a time, beating well after each addition, then beat in the orange rind and juice.

6 Gently fold in the flour mixture in batches, then spoon the batter into the prepared tin and tap gently to release any air bubbles. Bake for 35–40 minutes, or until the top of the cake is golden and springs back when pressed with the fingers.

7 Allow the cake to cool in the tin for 10 minutes, then turn it out on to a wire rack, remove the cake tin and leave to cool for a further 30 minutes. Slice and serve warm with a little of the fruit sauce. Decorate with the reserved fruit.

Nutritional information per portion: Energy 366kcal/ 1533kJ; Protein 5.4g; Carbohydrate 42.7g, of which sugars 26.1g; Fat 20.5g, of which saturates 12.1g; Cholesterol 118mg; Calcium 71mg; Fibre 2.1g; Sodium 163mg.

Lady Baltimore cake

This recipe was published in the 19th-century novel Lady Baltimore *by Owen Wister. The cake is a sponge that is covered with a fluffy white frosting that includes pecan nuts, figs and raisins. Make it for a special tea-time treat – it looks quite impressive. Store it for up to three days.*

SERVES 10–12

250ml/8fl oz/1 cup vegetable oil, plus extra
   for greasing
275g/10oz/2½ cups plain
   (all-purpose) flour
12.5ml/2½ tsp baking powder
4 eggs
350g/12oz/1¾ cups caster (superfine) sugar
grated rind of 1 large orange
250ml/8fl oz/1 cup fresh orange juice

FOR THE FROSTING
2 egg whites
350g/12oz/1¾ cups caster (superfine) sugar
1.25ml/¼ tsp cream of tartar
5ml/1 tsp vanilla extract
50g/2oz/½ cup pecan nuts, finely chopped
85g/3oz/generous ½ cup raisins, chopped
3 ready-to-eat dried figs, finely chopped
18 pecan halves, to decorate

1 Preheat the oven to 180°C/350°F/Gas 4. Grease and line two 23cm/9in round shallow cake tins (pans) with baking parchment.

2 In a bowl, sift together the flour and baking powder. Set aside.

3 Beat the eggs and sugar in another large bowl, using an electric whisk, until thick and pale. Beat in the orange rind and juice, then add the vegetable oil and mix well. On a low speed, beat in the flour mixture in three batches.

4 Divide the batter between the tins. Bake for 30 minutes, or until a skewer inserted in to the centre comes out clean. Stand for 15 minutes, then run a knife around the inside of the tins, and transfer the cakes to a rack to cool. Remove the lining.

5 To make the filling and topping, put the egg whites, sugar, 75ml/5 tbsp cold water and the cream of tartar in the top of a double boiler, or in a large heatproof bowl set over a pan of boiling water. Beat the mixture, using an electric whisk, until glossy and thick. Remove the pan from the heat, add the vanilla extract and beat until thick. Fold in the nuts, raisins and figs.

6 Spread a layer of the frosting on top of one cake. Sandwich with the second cake. Spread the top and sides with the remainder of the frosting, then arrange the pecan halves on top.

Nutritional information per portion: Energy 529kcal/2229kJ; Protein 5.9g; Carbohydrate 90.2g, of which sugars 74.3g; Fat 18.6g, of which saturates 2.2g; Cholesterol 63mg; Calcium 107mg; Fibre 1.9g; Sodium 51mg.

Angel food cake

Similar to a whisked sponge cake, the texture of this American classic is springy but slightly sticky, and the colour is snowy white. The cream of tartar helps to aerate the egg whites, and the addition of sugar creates a light meringue mixture. This cake will keep in the refrigerator for up to five days.

SERVES 20

65g/2½oz/9 tbsp plain (all-purpose) flour
15ml/1 tbsp cornflour (cornstarch)
225g/8oz/generous 1 cup caster
   (superfine) sugar
10 egg whites
5ml/1 tsp cream of tartar
7.5ml/1½ tsp vanilla extract

FOR THE FROSTING

2 egg whites
115g/4oz/generous ½ cup caster
   (superfine) sugar
10ml/2 tsp golden (light corn) syrup
2.5ml/½ tsp vanilla extract
rind of 1 orange, to decorate

1 Preheat the oven to 180°C/350°F/Gas 4. In a large bowl, sift together the flour, cornflour and 50g/2oz/¼ cup of the sugar three times, so that the texture is very, very light.

2 Put the egg whites and the cream of tartar into a clean, grease-free bowl and whisk until they form stiff peaks. Gradually whisk in the remaining sugar, 15ml/1 tbsp at a time, until the mixture becomes thick and glossy.

3 Using a metal spoon, gently fold the sifted flour and the vanilla extract into the whisked egg whites until combined. Transfer the mixture to a 25cm/10in non-stick ring mould and smooth out the batter so that it is level. Bake for 35–40 minutes, or until risen and golden. Remove from the oven, invert the cake in its mould on to a wire rack. Leave to go cold.

4 To make the frosting, put the egg whites into a clean, grease-free bowl. Whisk until stiff and dry, then set aside. Heat the sugar and 60ml/4 tbsp water in a small pan, stirring constantly until the sugar dissolves. Increase the heat and boil until the temperature reaches 115°C/240°F on a sugar thermometer. As soon as this temperature is reached, remove the pan from the heat.

5 Pour the syrup into the egg whites, whisking constantly, until the mixture is thick and glossy. Beat in the golden syrup and vanilla, beating for 5 minutes. Lift the mould off the cake and put the cake on a serving plate. Quickly spread the frosting over the cake. Sprinkle with orange rind.

Nutritional information per portion: Energy 117kcal/500kJ; Protein 3.1g; Carbohydrate 27.7g, of which sugars 21.4g; Fat 0.1g, of which saturates 0g; Cholesterol 0mg; Calcium 24mg; Fibre 0.3g; Sodium 49mg.

Madeira cake

This fine-textured cake is a good choice for a birthday or celebration cake, as it is firm but light, which makes it the perfect base for decorating. It is ideal to serve with hot drinks, either as it is or split and sandwiched with buttercream. Store for up to one week in an airtight container.

SERVES 8–10

175g/6oz/¾ cup butter, softened, plus
   extra for greasing
175g/6oz/scant 1 cup caster
   (superfine) sugar
3 eggs
15ml/1 tbsp lemon juice
225g/8oz/2 cups plain (all-purpose) flour
7.5ml/1½ tsp baking powder

1 Preheat the oven to 160°C/325°F/ Gas 3. Grease and line an 18cm/7in round deep cake tin (pan) with baking parchment.

2 In a large bowl, beat the butter and sugar together until light and fluffy, then beat in the eggs one at a time, beating well after each addition. Stir in the lemon juice.

3 Sift in the flour and baking powder and stir to combine.

4 Spoon the mixture into the prepared tin and smooth the top level with the back of the spoon.

5 Bake in the centre of the oven for 1¼–1½ hours, until golden, or until a skewer inserted into the centre comes out clean.

6 Leave the cake to cool in the tin for 45 minutes, then turn out on to a wire rack to go cold. Remove the lining paper.

Nutritional information per portion: Energy 453kcal/ 1894kJ; Protein 6.1g; Carbohydrate 51.4g, of which sugars 30g; Fat 26.3g, of which saturates 15.5g; Cholesterol 155mg; Calcium 74mg; Fibre 0.9g; Sodium 208mg.

Lemon drizzle cake

Wonderfully moist and lemony, this cake is a favourite at coffee mornings and for afternoon tea. A lemon and sugar syrup is poured over the cooked cake and allowed to soak through, so that the whole cake is sweet and tangy. It can be stored in an airtight container for up to five days.

SERVES 6–8

225g/8oz/1 cup unsalted butter,
    softened, plus extra for greasing
finely grated rind of 2 lemons
175g/6oz/scant 1 cup caster (superfine)
    sugar, plus 5ml/1 tsp
4 eggs
225g/8oz/2 cups self-raising
    (self-rising) flour
5ml/1 tsp baking powder
shredded rind of 1 lemon, to decorate

FOR THE SYRUP
juice of 1 lemon
150g/5oz/¾ cup caster (superfine) sugar

1 Preheat the oven to 160°C/325°F/ Gas 3. Grease and line the base and sides of an 18–20cm/7–8in round deep cake tin (pan) with baking parchment.

2 Mix the grated lemon rind and sugar together in a bowl.

3 In a large bowl, beat the butter with the lemon and sugar mixture until light and fluffy, then beat in the eggs one at a time.

4 Sift the flour and baking powder into the mixture in three batches and beat well.

5 Turn the batter into the prepared tin and smooth the top level. Bake for 1½ hours, or until golden brown and springy to the touch.

6 To make the syrup, slowly heat the juice with the sugar until dissolved.

7 Prick the top of the cake with a skewer and pour over the syrup. Sprinkle over the shredded lemon rind and 5ml/1 tsp sugar, then leave to cool. Remove the lining paper.

Nutritional information per portion: Energy 659kcal/ 2765kJ; Protein 8g; Carbohydrate 84.1g, of which sugars 56.2g; Fat 34.8g, of which saturates 21.4g; Cholesterol 213mg; Calcium 184mg; Fibre 1.2g; Sodium 466mg.

Lemon-and-lime cake

This cake has a lime syrup poured over the baked lemon sponge. It's perfect for busy cooks, and there is no need for icing. Keep this cake for up to three days in an airtight container.

SERVES 8

225g/8oz/1 cup butter, softened, plus
   extra for greasing
225g/8oz/2 cups self-raising
   (self-rising) flour
5ml/1 tsp baking powder
225g/8oz/generous 1 cup caster
   (superfine) sugar
4 eggs, beaten
grated rind of 2 lemons
30ml/2 tbsp lemon juice

FOR THE TOPPING
finely pared rind of 1 lime
juice of 2 limes
150g/5oz/¾ cup caster (superfine) sugar

1 Preheat the oven to 160°C/325°F/Gas 3. Grease and line a 20cm/8in round deep cake tin (pan) with baking parchment.

2 Sift the flour and baking powder into a large bowl. Add the sugar, butter and eggs, then beat together for 2 minutes until the mixture is smooth and fluffy. Use an electric mixer for speed, if you like. Beat in the lemon rind and juice. Turn the mixture into the prepared tin, smooth the top and make a shallow indentation in the centre.

3 Bake for 1¼–1½ hours, or until the cake is golden on top, and a skewer inserted into the centre comes out clean. Meanwhile, make the topping by mixing all the ingredients together in a bowl.

4 As soon as the cake is baked, pour over the topping. Leave to stand on a wire rack and let the cake cool in the tin. Remove the lining paper when cold.

Nutritional information per portion: Energy 527kcal/2209kJ; Protein 6.2g; Carbohydrate 71g, of which sugars 49.6g; Fat 26.3g, of which saturates 15.5g; Cholesterol 155mg; Calcium 84mg; Fibre 0.9g; Sodium 209mg.

Cherry cake

Both dried and glacé cherries are used in this elegant cake, which has the delicate flavour of almonds. Store in an airtight container for up to five days. Freeze, undecorated, for two months.

SERVES 10

175g/6oz/³⁄₄ cup unsalted butter, softened, plus extra for greasing

175g/6oz/scant 1 cup caster (superfine) sugar

3 eggs, beaten

150g/5oz/1¹⁄₄ cups self-raising (self-rising) flour

50g/2oz/¹⁄₂ cup plain (all-purpose) flour

75g/3oz/³⁄₄ cup each ground almonds and glacé (candied) cherries, washed

25g/1oz dried cherries

a few drops of almond extract

FOR THE DECORATION

115g/4oz/1 cup icing (confectioners') sugar, sifted

5ml/1 tsp lemon juice

50g/2oz/¹⁄₂ cup flaked (sliced) almonds

10 natural glacé (candied) cherries

1 Preheat the oven to 160°C/325°F/Gas 3. Grease and line a 20cm/8in round deep cake tin (pan).

2 In a bowl, beat the butter with the sugar until light and fluffy, using an electric whisk. Add the eggs a little at a time, with 5ml/1 tsp of flour. Sift in the flours, the ground almonds and cherries. Stir well. Add the flour and cherry mixture to the butter and sugar and fold together with the almond extract until smooth. Spoon into the cake tin and smooth level.

3 Bake for 45–50 minutes, or until a skewer inserted comes out clean. Cool slightly, then turn on to a wire rack to go cold. Remove the lining paper.

4 In a bowl, mix the icing sugar with the lemon juice, and 10–15ml/ 2–3 tsp water, to make a soft icing. Drizzle half over the cake top. Toast the almonds and sprinkle them into the centre. Place the cherries around the edge. Drizzle over the remaining icing.

Nutritional information per portion: Energy 367kcal/1535kJ; Protein 5g; Carbohydrate 43.7g, of which sugars 26.6g; Fat 20.4g, of which saturates 12g; Cholesterol 118mg; Calcium 75mg; Fibre 0.9g; Sodium 309mg.

Boston cream pie

*Created at the Parker House Hotel in Boston, in the 1850s, this famous 'pie' is actually a cake.
Sandwiched between the two cake layers is a rich custard. Keep, refrigerated, for up to three days.*

SERVES 8

butter, for greasing
225g/8oz/2 cups plain (all-purpose) four
15ml/1 tbsp baking powder
pinch of salt
115g/4oz/¹/₂ cup butter, softened
200g/7oz/1 cup caster (superfine) sugar
2 eggs
5ml/1 tsp vanilla extract
6fl oz/175ml/³/₄ cup milk

FOR THE FILLING
8fl oz/250ml/1 cup milk
3 egg yolks

90g/3¹/₂oz/¹/₂ cup caster (superfine) sugar
25g/1oz/¹/₄ cup plain (all-purpose) flour
15ml/1 tbsp butter
5ml/1 tsp vanilla extract

FOR THE CHOCOLATE GLAZE
25g/1oz dark (bittersweet) chocolate
15g/¹/₂oz/1 tbsp butter
50g/2oz/¹/₂ cup icing (confectioners') sugar,
   plus extra for dusting
2.5ml/¹/₂ tsp vanilla extract
15ml/1 tbsp hot water

1 Preheat the oven to 190°C/375°F/Gas 5. Grease and line two 20cm/8in round shallow cake tins (pans) with baking parchment.

2 Sift the flour with the baking powder and salt into a large bowl.

3 In a large bowl, beat the butter and sugar together until light and fluffy. Beat in the eggs one at a time, beating well after each addition. Stir in the vanilla extract.

4 Add the milk and the dry ingredients, alternating the batches and mixing only enough to blend. Divide the cake batter between the prepared tins and spread it out evenly.

5 Bake for 25 minutes, or until a skewer inserted into the centre comes out clean. Allow to stand in the tins for 5 minutes before turning out on to a wire rack to cool completely. Remove the lining.

6 To make the filling, heat the milk to boiling point in a small pan, and remove from the heat.

7 In a heatproof bowl, beat the egg yolks until smooth. Add the sugar and continue beating until pale yellow, then beat in the flour. While beating, pour the hot milk into the egg yolk mixture.

8 When all the milk has been added, put the bowl over a pan of boiling water. Heat, stirring constantly, until thickened. Cook for 2 minutes more, then remove from the heat. Stir in the butter and vanilla extract. Leave to cool.

9 Slice off the domed top of each cake to create a flat surface, if necessary. Put one cake on a serving plate and spread on the filling in a thick layer. Set the other cake on top, cut side down. Smooth the edge of the filling layer so that it is flush with the sides of the cake layers.

10 To make the chocolate glaze, melt the chocolate and butter in a heatproof bowl set over a pan of simmering water. Stir well. When smooth, remove from the heat and beat in the icing sugar using a wooden spoon. Add the vanilla extract, then beat in a little hot water to give a spreadable consistency. Spread evenly over the top of the cake. When it is set, dust the top with icing sugar.

Nutritional information per portion: Energy 499kcal/2100kJ; Protein 6g; Carbohydrate 77.1g, of which sugars 53.1g; Fat 20.3g, of which saturates 12.1g; Cholesterol 146mg; Calcium 112mg; Fibre 1g; Sodium 297mg.

Frosted walnut layer cake

Walnuts go very well in rich cakes, especially when combined with a sweet filling. This moist and nutty cake is layered with vanilla buttercream and then topped with swirls of light and fluffy frosting. It is ideal for a special party. Keep the cake for five days in an airtight container.

SERVES 12

225g/8oz/1 cup butter, softened, plus extra
    for greasing
225g/8oz/2 cups self-raising (self-rising) flour
5ml/1 tsp baking powder
225g/8oz/1 cup soft light brown sugar
75g/3oz/³/₄ cup walnuts, finely chopped
4 eggs
15ml/1 tbsp treacle (molasses)

FOR THE BUTTERCREAM
75g/3oz/6 tbsp unsalted butter
5ml/1 tsp vanilla extract
175g/6oz/1¹/₂ cups icing
    (confectioners') sugar

FOR THE MERINGUE FROSTING
2 large (US extra large) egg whites
350g/12oz/1³/₄ cups golden caster
    (superfine) sugar
pinch of salt
pinch of cream of tartar
15ml/1 tbsp warm water
whole walnut halves, to decorate

1 Preheat the oven to 160°C/325°F/Gas 3. Grease and line two 20cm/8in round shallow cake tins (pans) with baking parchment.

2 Sift the flour and baking powder into a large bowl, then add all the remaining ingredients.

3 Beat together for 2 minutes, or until smooth, then divide between the tins and spread level.

4 Bake for 25 minutes, or until golden and springy to the touch in the centre.

5 Allow to stand for 5 minutes, then turn out on to a wire rack to go cold. Remove the lining papers. Cut each cake in half horizontally using a long-bladed sharp knife.

6 To make the buttercream, in a large bowl, beat the butter, vanilla extract and icing sugar together until light and fluffy.

7 Spread a third thinly over one sponge half and place a sponge layer on top, then continue layering the sponges with the buttercream. Put the cake on to a serving plate.

8 To make the frosting, put the egg whites in a large heatproof bowl and add the caster sugar, salt, cream of tartar and water. Put the bowl over a pan of hot water and whisk with an electric mixer for 7 minutes, or until the mixture is thick and stands in peaks.

9 Immediately, use a metal spatula to swirl the frosting over the top and sides of the cake.

10 Arrange the walnut halves on top and leave to set for 10 minutes before serving.

Nutritional information per portion: Energy 563kcal/2349kJ; Protein 8.5g; Carbohydrate 50.6g, of which sugars 39.2g; Fat 35.3g, of which saturates 10.1g; Cholesterol 108mg; Calcium 114mg; Fibre 1.5g; Sodium 177mg.

Carrot cake with cream cheese icing

This cake is topped with a zesty orange and cream cheese icing, which goes perfectly with the nutty flavour of the cake. This cake will keep, refrigerated, for up to three days.

SERVES 10

120ml/4fl oz/¹/₂ cup sunflower oil, plus
   extra for greasing
90g/3¹/₂oz/scant 1 cup wholemeal (whole-
   wheat) flour
150g/5oz/1¹/₄ cups plain (all-purpose) flour
10ml/2 tsp baking powder
5ml/1 tsp bicarbonate of soda (baking soda)
5ml/1 tsp ground cinnamon
2.5ml/¹/₂ tsp ground allspice
250g/9oz/1¹/₄ cups soft light brown sugar
3 carrots, peeled and coarsely grated
115g/4oz/1 cup chopped walnuts

3 large eggs
juice of 1 orange
shreds of pared orange rind, to decorate

FOR THE ICING
50g/2oz/¹/₄ cup butter, softened
200g/7oz/scant 1 cup cream
   cheese, softened
grated rind of 1 orange
200g/7oz/1³/₄ cups icing
   (confectioners') sugar
5ml/1 tsp vanilla extract

1 Preheat the oven to 180°C/350°F/Gas 4. Grease and line a 23cm/9in round deep cake tin (pan) with baking parchment.

2 Sift the flours, baking powder, bicarbonate of soda, cinnamon and allspice into a bowl, then add the bran from the sieve (strainer). Add the brown sugar, carrots and walnuts. Make a well in the centre.

3 In another bowl, beat together the eggs and orange juice. Add the egg mixture with the remaining oil to the dry ingredients. Mix well. Spoon the batter into the prepared tin and level the top. Bake for about 1 hour, or until risen and springy to the touch.

4 Leave the cake in the tin on a wire rack for 10 minutes. Slide a knife between the cake and the tin to loosen it. Turn the cake out on to a rack and remove the lining paper. Leave to go cold.

5 To make the icing, beat the butter, cream cheese and orange rind in a bowl. Sift the icing sugar, then gradually add to the bowl with the vanilla extract. Beat well after each addition, until creamy. Spread the icing on top of the cake. Sprinkle the orange rind over the top of the iced cake to decorate.

Nutritional information per portion: Energy 397kcal/1664kJ; Protein 7.6g; Carbohydrate 49.2g, of which sugars 29.5g; Fat 20.3g, of which saturates 8.5g; Cholesterol 88mg; Calcium 75mg; Fibre 1.8g; Sodium 99mg.

Fruit Cakes

With their complex mixture of warm spices and succulent dried raisins, sultanas, and currants, traditional fruit cakes have a comforting flavour and aroma. They can be kept for up to four weeks in an airtight container. Lighter cakes made with fresh fruit, such as Streusel-topped Peach Cake or Pear and Polenta Cake, double up as puddings, and are lovely eaten the day they are baked while still warm and fresh, served with custard or whipped cream.

Griestorte with pineapple filling

This classic continental gateau uses semolina and ground almonds for a deliciously short, crunchy texture. Bake the base a day ahead, or bake and freeze it unfilled. Eat fresh once filled.

SERVES 8

butter, for greasing

3 eggs, separated

115g/4oz/generous 1/2 cup caster
  (superfine) sugar

juice and finely grated rind of 1/2 lemon

30ml/2 tbsp ground almonds

50g/2oz/1/3 cup fine semolina

icing (confectioners') sugar, for dusting

chocolate curls or flakes, to decorate

FOR THE FILLING

300ml/1/2 pint/11/2 cups double
  (heavy) cream

4 slices canned pineapple, drained and
  chopped

75g/3oz dark (bittersweet) chocolate,
  coarsely grated

1 Preheat the oven to 180°C/350°F/Gas 4. Grease and line a 20cm/8in round deep cake tin (pan) with baking parchment.

2 Whisk the egg yolks with the sugar and lemon rind until pale and light. Add the lemon juice. Whisk until thick and the mixture leaves a ribbon trail when the whisk is lifted. Fold in the almonds and semolina.

3 Whisk the egg whites until they form soft peaks, then fold into the yolk mixture in three batches. Spoon into the tin and bake for 30–35 minutes. Cool in the tin then turn the cake out on to a wire rack and cool completely. Remove the papers. Cut the cake in half horizontally.

4 Whip the cream, then fold in the pineapple and chocolate. Sandwich the cakes with the cream, dust with icing sugar, then decorate with chocolate curls.

Nutritional information per portion: Energy 356kcal/1484kJ; Protein 5g; Carbohydrate 29.7g, of which sugars 24.2g; Fat 27.2g, of which saturates 13.6g; Cholesterol 121mg; Calcium 52mg; Fibre 0.5g; Sodium 44mg.

Plum kuchen

Make this spicy cake when luscious plums are in season and at their sweetest and juiciest. Serve with a dollop of thick crème fraîche. Eat this fresh on the day it is baked.

SERVES 10

275g/10oz/2½ cups self-raising (self-rising) flour
7.5ml/1½ tsp ground cinnamon
115g/4oz/½ cup butter, diced
115g/4oz/½ cup soft light brown sugar
finely grated rind and juice of 1 small orange
2 eggs, beaten
60ml/4 tbsp milk
6 large, ripe dark plums, stoned (pitted) and quartered
30ml/2 tbsp demerara (raw) sugar
45ml/3 tbsp caster (superfine) sugar, to sprinkle

1 Preheat the oven to 180°C/350°F/Gas 4. Line the base and sides of a 20cm/8in deep round cake tin (pan) with baking parchment.

2 Sift the flour and 5ml/1 tsp cinnamon into a bowl and add the butter. Rub the butter into the flour until the mixture resembles fine crumbs. Stir in the soft light brown sugar and orange rind. Add the eggs and milk, and beat until smooth. Spoon into the tin. Arrange the plum pieces over the top of the cake, pressing them down slightly so that the fruit is half-covered by the mixture.

3 Sprinkle the cake with orange juice, demerara sugar and the remaining cinnamon. Bake for 1 hour or until a skewer inserted into the centre comes out clean. Cool in the tin for 5 minutes, then turn out to cool. Sprinkle with sugar.

Nutritional information per portion: Energy 311kcal/1308kJ; Protein 6.4g; Carbohydrate 44.5g, of which sugars 15.9g; Fat 13.2g, of which saturates 7.4g; Cholesterol 89mg; Calcium 86mg; Fibre 2.4g; Sodium 102mg.

Streusel-topped peach cake

If fresh summer fruits are not available, you can use canned peaches from the store cupboard. It also works well with canned apricots or black cherries. Serve fresh with thick cream.

SERVES 8–10

75g/3oz/6 tbsp butter, softened, plus
   extra for greasing
225g/8oz/2 cups self-raising
   (self-rising) flour
5ml/1 tsp baking powder
2.5ml/¹⁄₂ tsp ground cinnamon
75g/3oz/6 tbsp golden caster
   (superfine) sugar
finely grated rind of 1 orange
1 egg, beaten
150ml/¹⁄₄ pt/²⁄₃ cup milk

FOR THE TOPPING

75g/3oz/²⁄₃ cup self-raising
   (self-rising) flour
50g/2oz/¹⁄₂ cup unsalted butter, diced
25g/1oz/2 tbsp demerara (raw) sugar

FOR THE FILLING

400g/14oz can peach slices in
   juice, drained

1 Preheat the oven to 190°C/375°F/ Gas 5. Grease the base and sides of a 20cm/8in loose-based cake tin (pan) and line with baking parchment.

2 To make the topping, put the flour in a bowl or food processor, add the butter and process or rub in until fine crumbs form, then stir in the demerara sugar.

3 To make the cake, sift the flour, baking powder and cinnamon into a large bowl. Add all the remaining cake ingredients and beat together until mixed. Spoon into the tin then smooth the top level.

4 Cover the top with an even layer of drained peach slices. Sprinkle the crumb topping over the peaches.

5 Bake for 40 minutes, or until golden and a skewer inserted into the centre comes out clean.

6 Cool in the tin for 5 minutes, then carefully remove the sides of the tin and cool the cake on a wire rack. Remove the lining paper.

Nutritional information per portion: Energy 244kcal/ 1034kJ; Protein 4.7g; Carbohydrate 46.7g, of which sugars 39.4g; Fat 5g, of which saturates 0.8g; Cholesterol 71mg; Calcium 47mg; Fibre 0.9g; Sodium 32mg.

Gooseberry cake

Sugar and elderflower cordial are added to sweeten the gooseberries before they are added to the cake batter. Serve the cake fresh as a pudding with a spoonful of crème fraîche.

SERVES 10

75g/3oz/6 tbsp butter, melted, plus extra
   for greasing
150g/5oz gooseberries
22.5ml/4½ tsp golden caster
   (superfine) sugar
15ml/1 tbsp elderflower cordial, plus
   extra for brushing
225g/8oz/2 cups plain (all-purpose) flour
10ml/2 tsp baking powder
150g/5oz/¾ cup golden caster
   (superfine) sugar
2.5ml/½ tsp vanilla extract
1 egg, lightly beaten
250ml/8fl oz/1 cup buttermilk
icing (confectioners') sugar, for dusting

1 Preheat the oven to 180°C/350°F/ Gas 4. Lightly grease a 23cm/9in round loose-based cake tin (pan) with butter.

2 Arrange the fruit in a single layer on a plate and sprinkle evenly with the sugar and elderflower cordial. Leave to stand for 30 minutes.

3 Sift the dry ingredients into a large bowl and make a well in the centre.

4 In a separate bowl, lightly whisk together the melted butter, vanilla extract, egg and buttermilk. Pour into the dry ingredients and fold partly together.

5 Lightly combine half the reserved gooseberries and all of the syrupy juices into the batter, then fold together with a metal spoon.

6 Spoon the mixture into the tin and sprinkle the remaining fruit on top.

7 Bake for 30 minutes, but check after 25 minutes. If the centre of the cake is springy to the touch, it is ready. Lightly brush the surface of the warm cake with elderflower cordial, if you like, and serve, dusted with icing sugar.

Nutritional information per portion: Energy 273kcal/ 1144kJ; Protein 3.9g; Carbohydrate 34.6g, of which sugars 18.1g; Fat 14.2g, of which saturates 8.3g; Cholesterol 82mg; Calcium 51mg; Fibre 1g; Sodium 112mg.

Greek yogurt and fig cake

Fresh figs, thickly sliced then baked in honey, make a delectable base that becomes a topping for a featherlight sponge. Keep refrigerated in an airtight container for two days.

SERVES 8–10

200g/7oz/scant 1 cup butter, softened,
   plus extra for greasing
6 firm fresh figs, thickly sliced
45ml/3 tbsp clear honey, plus extra
   for glazing
175g/6oz/scant 1 cup caster
   (superfine) sugar
grated rind of 1 lemon
grated rind of 1 orange
4 eggs, separated
225g/8oz/2 cups plain (all-purpose) flour
5ml/1 tsp baking powder
5ml/1 tsp bicarbonate of soda
   (baking soda)
250ml/8fl oz/1 cup Greek (US strained
   plain) yogurt

1 Preheat the oven to 180C/350°F/Gas 4. Grease and line the base of a 23cm/9in cake tin (pan) with baking parchment. Arrange the sliced figs over the base of the tin and drizzle over the honey.

2 Beat the butter and sugar with the citrus rinds until pale and fluffy. Gradually beat in the egg yolks. Sift in the dry ingredients and yogurt in batches. Beat well, continue until both have been incorporated.

3 Put the egg whites into a clean, grease-free bowl and whisk until they form stiff peaks. Stir the egg whites into the cake batter in two batches. Pour the mixture over the figs in the tin and smooth the top level. Bake for 1¼ hours, or until a skewer inserted into the centre of the cake comes out clean.

4 Turn the cake out on to a wire rack, peel off the paper and cool. Drizzle the fig topping with extra honey before serving.

Nutritional information per portion: Energy 473kcal/1982kJ; Protein 8.2g; Carbohydrate 59.5g, of which sugars 38g; Fat 24.3g, of which saturates 14g; Cholesterol 149mg; Calcium 167mg; Fibre 2g; Sodium 225mg.

Crunchy-topped fresh apricot cake

Almonds are perfect partners for fresh apricots, and this is a great way to use fruits that are too firm for eating. Serve cold as a cake, or warm with custard for a dessert. It will keep for two days.

SERVES 8

175g/6oz/³/₄ cup butter, softened, plus
   extra for greasing
175g/6oz/1¹/₂ cups self-raising
   (self-rising) flour
175g/6oz/³/₄ cup caster (superfine) sugar
115g/4oz/1 cup ground almonds
3 eggs
5ml/1 tsp almond extract
2.5ml/¹/₂ tsp baking powder
8 firm apricots, stoned (pitted)
   and chopped

FOR THE TOPPING
30ml/2 tbsp demerara (raw) sugar
50g/2oz/¹/₂ cup flaked (sliced) almonds

1 Preheat the oven to 160°C/325°F/Gas 3. Grease and line an 18cm/7in round cake tin (pan) with baking parchment.

2 Put all the ingredients, except the apricots, in a large bowl or food processor and whisk or process until light and creamy. Fold the apricots into the cake batter. Spoon the batter into the prepared cake tin and smooth the top level. Make a hollow in the centre with the back of a large spoon.

3 Sprinkle over 15ml/1 tbsp of the demerara sugar, then scatter the almonds over the top. Bake for 1¹/₂ hours, or until a skewer inserted comes out clean.

4 Sprinkle the remaining demerara sugar over the top of the cake and leave to cool for 10 minutes in the tin. Remove from the tin, peel off the paper and finish cooling on a wire rack.

Nutritional information per portion: Energy 414kcal/1734kJ; Protein 6.2g; Carbohydrate 46.8g, of which sugars 30.3g; Fat 23.9g, of which saturates 12.3g; Cholesterol 118mg; Calcium 126mg; Fibre 1.8g; Sodium 241mg.

Apricot, prune and cherry cake

This moist cake has a tang of orange. As it stores well for several days, it's useful for tea-time treats during the week. It is one of the easiest cakes to make – just melt the basic ingredients together in a pan. Serve this sliced and buttered, if you like.

SERVES 8–10

175g/6oz/³/₄ cup butter, plus extra
   for greasing
175g/6oz/³/₄ cup soft dark muscovado
   (molasses) sugar
300ml/¹/₂ pint/1¹/₄ cups orange juice
130g/4¹/₂oz/generous ¹/₂ cup ready-to-
   eat dried apricots, chopped
130g/4¹/₂oz/generous ¹/₂ cup ready-to-
   eat prunes, chopped
125g/4¹/₄oz/ generous ¹/₂ cup glacé

(candied) cherries, washed, dried
   and chopped
50g/2oz/¹/₃ cup chopped mixed
   (candied) peel
250g/9oz/2¹/₄ cups plain
   (all-purpose) flour
2.5ml/¹/₂ tsp bicarbonate of soda
   (baking soda)
2 eggs, beaten
45ml/3 tbsp golden (light corn) syrup

1 Preheat the oven to 180°C/350°F/ Gas 4. Grease and line an 18cm/7in deep round cake tin (pan) with baking parchment.

2 Put the butter, sugar and orange juice in a pan and heat until the sugar dissolves. Add all the dried fruits, then simmer gently for 15 minutes. Leave to cool.

3 Sift the flour and bicarbonate of soda into the cooled fruit mixture with the beaten eggs.

4 Spoon into the tin and bake for 1¼ hours, until a skewer inserted into the centre of the cake comes out clean.

5 Leave to cool in the tin for 10 minutes, then turn out on to a wire rack, peel away the papers and cool.

6 Warm the golden syrup in a small pan, then brush it over the top of the cake to glaze before serving.

Nutritional information per portion: Energy 399kcal/ 1680kJ; Protein 5.6g; Carbohydrate 62g, of which sugars 43g; Fat 16.1g, of which saturates 9.8g; Cholesterol 78mg; Calcium 94mg; Fibre 3.7g; Sodium 182mg.

Pear and polenta cake

This light polenta sponge has a nutty corn flavour that complements the fruit perfectly. For this upside-down cake, pears and honey are added to the base of the cake tin, then the mixture is added on top. Serve as a dessert with custard or whipped cream, if you like. Eat fresh.

SERVES 10

butter, for greasing
175g/6oz/scant 1 cup golden caster
  (superfine) sugar
4 ripe pears, peeled and cored
juice of ¹/₂ lemon
30ml/2 tbsp clear honey
3 eggs
seeds from 1 vanilla pod (bean)
120ml/4fl oz/¹/₂ cup sunflower oil
115g/4oz/1 cup self-raising
  (self-rising) flour
50g/2oz/¹/₃ cup instant
  polenta (cornmeal)

1 Preheat the oven to 180°C/350°F/ Gas 4. Grease and line a 20cm/8in round cake tin (pan) with baking parchment.

2 Sprinkle 30ml/2 tbsp of the sugar over the base of the prepared tin.

3 Cut the pears into chunky slices and toss them in the lemon juice.

4 Arrange the pears on the base of the cake tin. Drizzle the honey over, and set aside.

5 In a bowl, mix together the eggs, the seeds from the vanilla pod and the remaining sugar. Beat until thick and creamy, then gradually beat in the oil.

6 Sift the flour and polenta into the egg mixture and fold in. Pour the batter over the pears in the tin.

7 Bake for 50 minutes, or until a skewer inserted into the centre comes out clean. Cool in the tin for 10 minutes, then turn the cake out, and peel off the lining paper.

COOK'S TIP
To release the seeds from the vanilla pod, cut down the centre with a sharp knife, then scoop out the seeds with a teaspoon.

Nutritional information per portion: Energy 256kcal/ 1077kJ; Protein 3.7g; Carbohydrate 38.9g, of which sugars 26.7g; Fat 10.5g, of which saturates 1.5g; Cholesterol 57mg; Calcium 65mg; Fibre 1.8g; Sodium 66mg.

Rich fruit cake

Use a food processor to chop and combine whole citrus fruits and dates to make this incredibly moist cake that is bursting with fruity and spicy flavours. This traditional cake is ideal for decorating for Christmas or special occasions. It will keep for one month in an airtight container.

SERVES 10–12

75g/3oz/scant 1/2 cup butter, plus extra
   for greasing
1 large orange, unpeeled, washed, cut into
   pieces and seeded
1 large lemon, unpeeled, washed, cut into
   pieces and seeded
1 large cooking apple, unpeeled, washed,
   cored and cut into pieces
90g/3 1/2 oz/generous 1/2 cup stoned
   (pitted) dates
75g/3oz/6 tbsp hazelnut butter
90g/3 1/2 oz/generous 1/2 cup raisins
90g/3 1/2 oz/generous 1/2 cup currants
90g/3 1/2 oz/generous 1/2 cup sultanas
   (golden raisins)

90g/3 1/2 oz/generous 1/2 cup ready-to-eat
   stoned (pitted) prunes, chopped
50g/2oz/1/2 cup cashew nut pieces
5ml/1 tsp ground cinnamon
5ml/1 tsp freshly grated nutmeg
2.5ml/1/2 tsp mace
2.5ml/1/2 tsp ground cloves
115g/4oz/1 cup wholemeal
   (whole-wheat) flour
7.5ml/1 1/2 tsp baking powder
115g/4oz/generous 1 cup rolled oats,
   processed until smooth
3 large (US extra large) eggs, beaten
45–60ml/3–4 tbsp unsweetened coconut
   milk, if needed

1 Preheat the oven to 150°F/300°C/Gas 2. Grease and line a 20cm/8in round deep cake tin (pan) with baking parchment.

2 Put the first six ingredients in a food processor and process to make a rough purée.

3 Scrape the mixture into a bowl and stir in the raisins, currants, sultanas, prunes, nuts and spices.

4 Stir in the flour, baking powder and oats, alternating with the eggs.

5 If the mixture seems very dry, stir in the coconut milk.

6 Spoon the batter into the prepared tin and smooth the top level. Bake for 1 hour, or until a skewer inserted into the centre comes out clean. Cool for 15 minutes, then turn out to cool on a wire rack.

Nutritional information per portion: Energy 376kcal/1576kJ; Protein 2.4g; Carbohydrate 52.4g, of which sugars 52.4g; Fat 18.4g, of which saturates 7.9g; Cholesterol 30mg; Calcium 54mg; Fibre 1.2g; Sodium 123mg.

Farmhouse apple and sultana cake

This is a traditional, flavourful country cake made very simply and easily using the creaming method. It has a sweet, crispy top, a lovely moist texture and a spicy apple flavour – it makes an ideal tea-time treat. Keep this cake for 2 days in an airtight container in a cool place.

SERVES 12

175g/6oz/¾ cup softened butter, plus
    extra for greasing
175g/6oz/¾ cup soft light brown sugar
3 eggs
225g/8oz/2 cups self-raising (self-rising)
    flour, sifted
5ml/1 tsp baking powder, sifted

10ml/2 tsp mixed (apple pie) spice
350g/12oz cooking apples, peeled, cored
    and diced
175g/6oz/generous 1 cup sultanas
    (golden raisins)
75ml/5 tbsp milk
30ml/2 tbsp demerara (raw) sugar

1 Preheat the oven to 160°C/325°F/ Gas 3. Grease and line a 20cm/8in round deep cake tin (pan) with baking parchment.

2 Put the butter in a large bowl with the sugar. Beat together until light and fluffy. Beat in the eggs. Sift in the flour, baking powder and spice, then beat until thoroughly mixed.

3 Fold in the apples, sultanas and sufficient milk to make a soft dropping consistency.

4 Spoon the batter into the prepared tin. Wet a metal spoon by running it under the tap and use the back of the wet spoon to smooth the cake top level.

5 Sprinkle with demerara sugar. Bake for about 1½ hours, or until risen, golden brown and firm to the touch. Cool in the tin for 5 minutes, then turn out on to a wire rack.

Nutritional information per portion: Energy 310kcal/ 1305kJ; Protein 4.2g; Carbohydrate 45.5g, of which sugars 31.2g; Fat 13.7g, of which saturates 8.4g; Cholesterol 81mg; Calcium 63mg; Fibre 1.3g; Sodium 135mg.

Kugelhupf

A special fluted ring mould with a chimney in the middle is a traditional tool of Austrian bakers. These tins can be used to bake rich yeasted mixtures, or this light almond sponge, which is spectacular when decorated with icing, nuts and fruits. Keep for five days in an airtight container.

SERVES 12

225g/8oz/1 cup unsalted butter, softened (plus extra melted butter for greasing)
225g/8oz/generous 1 cup caster (superfine) sugar
3 eggs
225g/8oz/2 cups self-raising (self-rising) flour
finely grated rind of 1 orange
50g/2oz/1/3 cup chopped mixed peel
25g/1oz/1/4 cup dried cranberries or dried cherries
50g/2oz/1/3 cup sultanas (golden raisins)
50g/2oz/1/4 cup whole almonds, chopped
15ml/1 tbsp milk

FOR THE TOPPING AND ICING

45ml/3 tbsp clear honey
60ml/4 tbsp orange juice
115g/4oz/1 cup icing (confectioners') sugar
15ml/1 tbsp orange juice
15ml/1 tbsp dried cranberries or cherries
30ml/2 tbsp whole almonds, halved
15ml/1 tbsp whole dried orange and lemon peel, chopped

1 Preheat the oven to 190°C/375°F/ Gas 5. Brush a 1.75 litre/3 pint/ 7½ cup Kugelhupf mould well with melted butter.

2 In a bowl, beat together the butter and sugar. Beat in the eggs, adding 5ml/1 tsp flour with each egg.

3 Sift in the flour, then fold in with the orange rind, peel, cranberries, sultanas, almonds and milk.

4 Spoon into the tin and level the top. Bake for about 1 hour. Cool in the tin for 5 minutes, then turn out to cool on a wire rack.

5 For the topping, put the honey and orange juice in a small pan and heat gently until the honey melts. Brush over the cake. Leave to cool.

6 Sift the icing sugar into a large bowl, then blend with the orange juice. Spoon the icing over the cake, allowing it to drizzle down the sides. Sprinkle the cranberries or cherries, almonds and orange and lemon peel decoratively around the top of the cake then leave to set before serving.

Nutritional information per portion: Energy 319kcal/ 1339kJ; Protein 7g; Carbohydrate 41.8g, of which sugars 14.6g; Fat 14.6g, of which saturates 5.8g; Cholesterol 68mg; Calcium 87mg; Fibre 1.9g; Sodium 83mg.

Flourless fruit cake

Here's a really easy recipe that everyone will enjoy making. Instead of flour, the mixture contains cornflakes, so children can have fun crushing them and stirring the ingredients together. It is packed with fruity flavours too, from mincemeat to soft ready-to-eat figs.

SERVES 12–15

butter, for greasing
450g/1lb/1¼ cups mincemeat
350g/12oz/2 cups dried mixed fruit
115g/4oz/1 cup ready-to-eat dried
    apricots, chopped
115g/4oz/1 cup ready-to-eat dried
    figs, chopped
115g/4oz/½ cup glacé (candied)
    cherries, halved
115g/4oz/1 cup walnut pieces
225g/8oz/8–10 cups cornflakes, crushed
4 eggs, lightly beaten
400g/14oz can evaporated milk
5ml/1 tsp mixed (apple pie) spice
5ml/1 tsp baking powder
glacé (candied) fruits, chopped, to decorate

1 Preheat the oven to 150°C/300°F/Gas 2. Grease and line the base and sides of a 25cm/10in round cake tin (pan) with baking parchment.

2 Put all the ingredients into a large bowl and beat together well. Spoon into the prepared tin and smooth the top level.

COOK'S TIPS
To crush the cornflakes, put them in a plastic bag and tap with a rolling pin.

3 Bake in the centre of the oven for 1¾ hours, or until a skewer inserted into the centre of the cake comes out clean.

4 Cool in the tin for about 10 minutes, then turn out to cool on a wire rack. Peel off the lining paper and leave on the wire rack to cool completely.

5 Sprinkle with the chopped glacé fruits to decorate.

Nutritional information per portion: Energy 350kcal/1479kJ; Protein 7.4g; Carbohydrate 62.6g, of which sugars 50.38g; Fat 9.5g, of which saturates 1.5g; Cholesterol 56mg; Calcium 141mg; Fibre 2.4g; Sodium 224mg.

Currant cake

This traditional currant cake, from Norway, known as tiesen lap, uses the rubbed-in method of cake-making for combining the butter with the dry ingredients. Rather like a teabread, this cake is flavoured with nutmeg, and is light and moist with a crisp crust. It will keep for three days.

SERVES 10–12

130g/4¹/₂oz/9 tbsp butter, diced, plus
    extra for greasing
250g/9oz/2¹/₄ cups plain
    (all-purpose) flour
7.5ml/1¹/₂ tsp baking powder
2.5ml/¹/₂ tsp freshly grated nutmeg
130g/4¹/₂oz/scant ³/₄ cup caster
    (superfine) sugar
130g/4¹/₂oz/¹/₂ cup currants or sultanas
    (golden raisins)
2 eggs, lightly beaten
150ml/¹/₄ pint/²/₃ cup milk or buttermilk

1 Preheat the oven to 190°C/375°F/ Gas 5. Grease a shallow 20cm/8in round cake tin (pan).

2 Sift the flour, baking powder and nutmeg into a large bowl and stir in the sugar.

3 Add the butter and, with cold fingertips, rub the butter into the flour until the mixture resembles fine breadcrumbs. Stir in the currants or sultanas.

4 Stir in the eggs with enough milk or buttermilk to make a soft dropping consistency.

5 Spoon the batter into the prepared tin and smooth the top level.

6 Bake for 30–40 minutes, or until risen, golden brown and cooked through, and a skewer inserted in the centre comes out clean. Cool in the tin for 5 minutes, then turn out to go cold on a wire rack.

Nutritional information per portion: Energy 283kcal/1190kJ; Protein 4.5g; Carbohydrate 41.9g, of which sugars 22.8g; Fat 12g, of which saturates 7g; Cholesterol 65mg; Calcium 73mg; Fibre 1g; Sodium 105mg.

Caribbean rum cake

This marvellously moist fruit cake is filled with tropical fruits – pineapple, papaya and mango – that have been soaked in rum. It is sweet and spicy with a fruity, coconut topping. Start preparations the day before for the best results. Keep this for five days in an airtight container.

SERVES 10–12

50g/2oz/scant ⅓ cup sultanas
    (golden raisins)
175g/6oz/1 cup ready-to-eat dried
    pineapple, chopped
175g/6oz/1 cup ready-to-eat dried
    papaya, chopped
175g/6oz/1 cup ready-to-eat dried
    mango, chopped
60ml/4 tbsp rum
225g/8oz/1 cup butter, softened, plus
    extra for greasing
225g/8oz/1 cup soft light brown sugar

4 eggs, beaten
225g/8oz/2 cups plain (all-purpose) flour
10ml/2 tsp mixed (apple pie) spice

FOR THE TOPPING

75g/3oz/1 cup desiccated (dry
    unsweetened shredded) coconut
50g/2oz/⅓ cup ready-to-eat dried
    papaya, chopped
50g/2oz/⅓ cup ready-to-eat dried
    pineapple, chopped

1 Combine the sultanas with the dried pineapple, papaya and mango in a bowl. Spoon the rum over, then cover and leave for a few hours, or preferably overnight.

2 Preheat the oven to 180°C/350°F/ Gas 4. Grease and line a 20cm/8in round cake tin (pan) with baking parchment.

3 Cream the butter with the sugar. Beat in the eggs, a little at a time.

4 Sift over the flour and mixed spice, then fold in. Stir in the soaked fruits and mix thoroughly. Spoon into the cake tin and smooth the top level.

5 To make the topping, mix the coconut, papaya and pineapple in a small bowl. Sprinkle over the batter.

6 Bake for 1½–1¾ hours, or until a skewer inserted into the centre comes out clean. Cool in the tin for 15 minutes, then turn out on to a wire rack. Remove the lining paper.

Nutritional information per portion: Energy 434kcal/ 1826kJ; Protein 5.6g; Carbohydrate 63.2g, of which sugars 49.1g; Fat 18g, of which saturates 10.3g; Cholesterol 118mg; Calcium 86mg; Fibre 2.1g; Sodium 172mg.

Porter cake

Stout and porter are dark, full-flavoured beers and they can add real depth of flavour in cooking. This recipe originated in Ireland during the 19th century, where those drinks were popular, and it makes a fruit cake rich and tasty. Store this cake for one week before eating.

SERVES 10–12

225g/8oz/1 cup butter, at room
   temperature, plus extra for greasing
225g/8oz/1 cup soft dark brown sugar
350g/12oz/3 cups plain
   (all-purpose) flour
5ml/1 tsp baking powder
5ml/1 tsp mixed (apple pie) spice
3 eggs
450g/1lb/2⅓ cups mixed dried fruit
115g/4oz/½ cup glacé (candied) cherries
115g/4oz/⅔ cup mixed (candied) peel
50g/2oz/½ cup chopped almonds
   or walnuts
about 150ml/¼ pint/⅔ cup stout

1 Preheat the oven to 160°C/325°F/ Gas 3. Grease and line a 20cm/8in round cake tin (pan) with baking parchment.

2 In a large bowl, cream the butter and sugar with a wooden spoon until light and fluffy.

3 Sift the flour, baking powder and spice into another bowl.

4 Add the eggs to the butter and sugar mixture, beating well and adding 5ml/1 tsp of the flour mixture with each addition to prevent the batter from curdling. Mix well and fold in the remaining flour.

5 Add the dried fruit and nuts and enough stout to make a dropping consistency. Mix. Spoon into the tin and smooth the top level.

6 Bake for 1 hour. Reduce the heat to 150°C/300°F/Gas 2 and bake for another 1½–2 hours, or until a skewer inserted comes out clean. Allow to go cold in the tin.

7 Remove the lining paper, wrap in fresh baking parchment and store in an airtight container for about a week before eating.

Nutritional information per portion: Energy 510kcal/ 2150kJ; Protein 6.7g; Carbohydrate 80.4g, of which sugars 58g; Fat 20g, of which saturates 10.4g; Cholesterol 0.9mg; Calcium 0.1mg; Fibre 2.5g; Sodium 0.1mg.

Sugar-free fruit cake

Although this cake tastes sweet, it contains no added sugar – the sweetness comes from date purée and dried fruit. The cake is lower in calories than the average fruit cake.

SERVES 8–10

130g/4¹/₂oz/generous ¹/₂ cup softened
    butter, plus extra for greasing
175g/6oz/1 generous cup dried stoned
    (pitted) dates, chopped
finely grated rind of 1 small orange
225g/8oz/2 cups self-raising wholemeal
    (self-rising whole-wheat) flour
5ml/1 tsp mixed (apple pie) spice
3 eggs, beaten
450g/1lb/2²/₃ cups mixed dried fruit
25g/1oz/¹/₄ cup ground almonds
50g/2oz/¹/₂ cup flaked (sliced) almonds
15ml/1 tbsp clear honey, warmed,
    to glaze

1 Preheat the oven to 180°C/350°F/Gas 4. Grease and line a 20cm/8in round deep cake tin (pan) with baking parchment.

2 Put the dates in a heavy pan with the orange rind and 150ml/¹/₄ pint/²/₃ cup water. Simmer gently for 3–4 minutes, or until the dates form a purée, then leave to cool for 10 minutes.

3 Sift the flour and spice into a large bowl, then add the cooled purée and butter, eggs, dried fruit and ground almonds. Beat with a wooden spoon for about 3 minutes, or until light and fluffy. Spoon into the tin and smooth the top level. Sprinkle with the sliced almonds.

4 Bake for about 1¹/₄ hours, or until a skewer inserted into the centre comes out clean.

5 Brush the warmed melted honey lightly over the flaked almonds on top of the cake, for a shiny glaze. Leave to cool in the tin for 15 minutes, then turn out to go cold and peel away the paper. The cake keeps for two weeks.

Nutritional information per portion: Energy 406kcal/1709kJ; Protein 7.1g; Carbohydrate 60.1g, of which sugars 43.2g; Fat 17g, of which saturates 7.9g; Cholesterol 87mg; Calcium 148mg; Fibre 2.9g; Sodium 224mg.

All-in-one mixed fruit cake

Since the ingredients are added all at once, this cake is easy to make. Serve it plain or as a base for a celebration cake. Make it a week ahead to develop the flavour and improve the texture.

SERVES 8–10

175g/6oz/³⁄₄ cup butter, softened, plus
    extra for greasing
225g/8oz/2 cups self-raising
    (self-rising) flour
2.5ml/¹⁄₂ tsp mixed (apple pie) spice
175g/6oz/³⁄₄ cup muscovado
    (molasses) sugar
3 eggs, beaten
350g/12oz/2 cups luxury mixed
    dried fruit
50g/2oz/¹⁄₂ cup glacé (candied) cherries,
    washed, dried and chopped
15ml/1 tbsp treacle (molasses)

1 Preheat the oven to 160°C/325°F/Gas 3. Grease and line the base and sides of a deep 20cm/8in round cake tin (pan) with a double layer of baking parchment snipped at the bottom edge to make a neat seal.

2 Sift the flour and spice into a large bowl, then add all the remaining ingredients.

3 Beat with a wooden spoon for about 3 minutes, or until the mixture is well combined, thick and creamy. Spoon into the prepared tin and smooth the top level.

4 Bake for 2–2¼ hours, or until a skewer inserted into the centre comes out clean. Leave to cool in the tin for 15 minutes, then turn out to go cold on a wire rack.

Nutritional Information per portion: Energy 346kcal/1454kJ; Protein 4.3g; Carbohydrate 52.1g, of which sugars 39.1g; Fat 10.7g, of which saturates 6.2g; Cholesterol 62mg; Calcium 66mg; Fibre 2.1g; Sodium 90mg.

Mincemeat cake

If you have part of a jar of fruit mincemeat and a few small oranges left over after the Christmas holiday, they make a great basis for a tangy, quick and easy cake. Enrich the batter with some plain chocolate to make the cake even more special. Keep for one week in an airtight container.

SERVES 8–10

115g/4oz/½ cup soft tub margarine, plus extra for greasing

3 small oranges

75g/3oz/⅓ cup soft dark brown sugar

2 eggs, beaten

175g/6oz/1½ cups self-raising (self-rising) flour

2.5ml/½ tsp baking powder

15ml/1 tbsp milk

225g/8oz/⅔ cup luxury fruit mincemeat

50g/2oz plain (semisweet) chocolate, grated

FOR THE DECORATION

175g/6oz/1½ cups icing (confectioners') sugar

1 Preheat the oven to 160°C/325°F/Gas 3. Grease and line a 20cm/8in round deep cake tin (pan) with baking parchment.

2 Finely grate the rind from two oranges and put it in a large bowl.

3 Pare long shreds of peel from the third orange, then set aside.

4 Squeeze the juice from two oranges and keep 30ml/2 tbsp aside for the icing.

5 Put the remaining juice and all the other cake ingredients into a large bowl. Beat with a wooden spoon for about 2 minutes, or until the mixture is soft and smooth. Spoon into the tin and smooth the top level.

6 Bake for 40–45 minutes, or until firm and a warmed skewer inserted into the centre comes out clean. Cool in the tin for 10 minutes, then turn out to cool on a wire rack and peel away the papers.

7 To make the decoration, mix the icing sugar with the reserved orange juice until smooth. Spread over the top of the cold cake and allow the icing to run in drizzles down the sides. Sprinkle the orange shreds on top of the cake and leave to set for 30 minutes.

Nutritional information per portion: Energy 292kcal/1227kJ; Protein 2g; Carbohydrate 44.6g, of which sugars 44.4g; Fat 13g, of which saturates 7.9g; Cholesterol 66mg; Calcium 37mg; Fibre 0.5g; Sodium 135mg.

Vinegar cake

This fruit cake is sweet and moist, and not in the least sour from the white wine vinegar. It is made using an old-fashioned recipe, which contains no eggs, and the vinegar helps the mixture to rise. Keep in an airtight tin for one week and freeze whole or in slices for up to two months.

SERVES 12

150g/5oz/10 tbsp butter or block
   margarine, diced, plus extra
   for greasing
300g/11oz/2²⁄₃ cups plain
   (all-purpose) flour
150g/5oz/generous ¹⁄₂ cup soft dark
   brown sugar
75g/3oz/generous ³⁄₄ cup raisins
75g/3oz/³⁄₄ cup sultanas (golden raisins)
50g/2oz/¹⁄₃ cup chopped mixed
   (candied) peel
2.5ml/¹⁄₂ tsp bicarbonate of soda
   (baking soda)
250ml/8fl oz/1 cup milk
25ml/1¹⁄₂ tbsp white wine vinegar

1 Preheat the oven to 180°C/350°F/ Gas 4. Grease and line a 20cm/8in round deep cake tin (pan).

2 Sift the flour into a large bowl. Add the butter and rub in until the mixture resembles fine breadcrumbs. Add the sugar and dried fruits, and stir together.

3 Dissolve the bicarbonate of soda in 75ml/5 tbsp of the milk and add to the dry ingredients.

4 Stir the vinegar into the remaining milk and pour into the bowl.

5 Beat with a wooden spoon until smooth, then spoon into the prepared tin and smooth the top level. Indent the centre slightly.

Nutritional information per portion: Energy 276kcal/ 1159kJ; Protein 3.6g; Carbohydrate 43.4g, of which sugars 24.3g; Fat 11g, of which saturates 7g; Cholesterol 30mg; Calcium 78mg; Fibre 1.1g; Sodium 110mg.

6 Bake for 1 hour, then reduce the heat to 160°C/325°F/Gas 3 and bake for a further 20 minutes, or until a warmed skewer inserted into the centre comes out clean.

7 Cool in the tin for 5 minutes, then turn out to go cold on a wire rack.

Dundee cake

This classic Scottish fruit cake is decorated in the traditional way, topped with whole blanched almonds. Make in advance so the flavour can mature. Keep for one month in an airtight container.

SERVES 10–12

175g/6oz/³⁄₄ cup butter, plus extra
   for greasing
175g/6oz/³⁄₄ cup soft light brown sugar
3 eggs
225g/8oz/2 cups plain (all-purpose) flour
10ml/2 tsp baking powder
5ml/1 tsp ground cinnamon
2.5ml/¹⁄₂ tsp ground cloves
pinch of freshly grated nutmeg
225g/8oz/1¹⁄₂ cups sultanas
   (golden raisins)
175g/6oz/³⁄₄ cup glacé (candied) cherries
115g/4oz/²⁄₃ cup chopped mixed
   (candied) peel
50g/2oz/¹⁄₂ cup blanched almonds,
   roughly chopped
grated rind of 1 lemon
30ml/2 tbsp brandy
75g/3oz/³⁄₄ cup whole blanched
   almonds, to decorate

1 Preheat the oven to 160°C/325°F/Gas 3. Grease and line a 20cm/8in round deep cake tin (pan).

2 Beat the butter and sugar together in a bowl. Add each egg, beating thoroughly after each addition.

3 Sift the flour, baking powder and spices together. Fold into the creamed mixture, alternating with the remaining ingredients. Mix until evenly blended.

4 Spoon into the prepared tin and smooth the top level, then make a dip in the centre.

5 Decorate the top by arranging the whole almonds in decreasing circles over the entire surface. Bake in the preheated oven for 2–2¹⁄₄ hours, or until a skewer inserted into the centre comes out clean.

6 Cool in the tin for 30 minutes, then turn out to cool on a wire rack.

Nutritional information per portion: Energy 292kcal/1229kJ; Protein 4.37g; Carbohydrate 41.5g, of which sugars 32.8g; Fat 12.9g, of which saturates 5.2g; Cholesterol 47mg; Calcium 69mg; Fibre 1.7g; Sodium 91mg.

Spice, Nut and Seed Cakes

The flavour, aroma and piquancy of spices can transform even the simplest cakes. Cinnamon, ginger and cardamom bring a taste of the exotic to Pineapple and Ginger Upside-down Cake or Pear and Cardamom Spice Cake, which also has the crunchiness of walnuts. Ground almonds add a lovely soft texture and a delicious flavour to Moist Orange and Almond Cake, while Rich Lemon Poppy-seed Cake is tangy and light with a pleasing bite.

Cardamom cake

Warm-flavoured cardamom is a favourite spice among all the Scandinavian countries and it is used in many cakes. This cake will keep for up to five days in an airtight container.

SERVES 10

250g/9oz/generous 1 cup butter, softened, plus extra for greasing
375g/13oz/3¼ cups plain (all-purpose) flour
45ml/3 tbsp baking powder
10 cardamom pods, seeds removed and finely crushed
250g/9oz/1¼ cups caster (superfine) sugar
3 large (US extra large) eggs, lightly beaten
150ml/¼ pint/⅔ cup milk
45ml/3 tbsp raisins
45ml/3 tbsp candied peel
15ml/1 tbsp flaked (sliced) almonds

1 Preheat the oven to 190°C/375°F/ Gas 5. Grease and line a 1kg/2¼lb loaf tin (pan) with baking parchment.

2 Sift the flour, baking powder and crushed cardamom seeds together.

3 In a large bowl, cream together the butter and sugar until light and fluffy. Beat in the eggs one at a time, adding a teaspoon of the flour with each egg, then fold in the remaining flour.

4 Add the milk, a little at a time, folding in well after each addition.

5 Add the raisins, candied peel and almonds, and fold in well. Transfer the mixture to the tin and smooth the top with a spoon until it is level.

6 Bake for 50 minutes, or until the cake is risen and firm to the touch. Turn out and cool on a wire rack. Remove the lining paper before slicing.

Nutritional information per portion: Energy 389kcal/1619kJ; Protein 4.6g; Carbohydrate 34.9g, of which sugars 17.7g; Fat 26.6g, of which saturates 14.8g; Cholesterol 97mg; Calcium 61mg; Fibre 2g; Sodium 201mg.

Caraway seed cake

Just a few caraway seeds give this cake a delicately warm and spicy flavour that blends well with the tangy peel. This cake will keep for up to two days in an airtight container.

SERVES 8

175g/6oz/¾ cup butter, softened, plus
   extra for greasing
175g/6oz/scant 1 cup caster
   (superfine) sugar
3 eggs
225g/8oz/2 cups plain (all-purpose) flour
5ml/1 tsp baking powder
10ml/2 tsp caraway seeds
50g/2oz/⅓ cup finely chopped mixed
   (candied) peel
30ml/2 tbsp milk or buttermilk

1 Preheat the oven to 180°C/350°F/ Gas 4. Grease and line a 20cm/8in round deep cake tin (pan) with baking parchment.

2 In a bowl, beat the butter and sugar until fluffy, then beat in the eggs one at a time. Sift the flour with the baking powder into the bowl. Add the caraway seeds and milk. Beat well.

3 Using a metal spoon, fold in the remaining ingredients.

4 Spoon the batter into the prepared tin and smooth the top level. Bake for 1–1¼ hours, or until a skewer comes out clean.

5 Cool for 15 minutes in the tin, then turn out on to a wire rack to go cold. Remove the lining paper.

Nutritional information per portion: Energy 281kcal/1181kJ; Protein 4.6g; Carbohydrate 36.9g, of which sugars 15.5g; Fat 13.8g, of which saturates 8g; Cholesterol 87mg; Calcium 58mg; Fibre 0.8g; Sodium 109mg.

Lavender cake

The delicate flavour and fragrance of lavender makes a delightful addition to cooking and is most suitable for sweet baking. Make this scented moist cake for tea on a summer's day using fresh lavender, or dried culinary lavender. This cake will keep for up to three days in an airtight tin.

SERVES 8

175g/6oz/³⁄₄ cup unsalted butter, softened, plus extra for greasing
175g/6oz/scant 1 cup caster (superfine) sugar
3 eggs
175g/6oz/1¹⁄₂ cups self-raising (self-rising) flour
15ml/1 tbsp fresh lavender florets or dried culinary lavender, roughly chopped (see Cook's tip)

2.5ml/¹⁄₂ tsp vanilla extract
30ml/2 tbsp milk

FOR THE TOPPING
50g/2oz/¹⁄₂ cup icing (confectioners') sugar, sifted
fresh lavender florets, to decorate

1 Preheat the oven to 180°C/350°F/Gas 4. Grease and flour a 20cm/8in round deep cake tin (pan).

2 In a large bowl, cream the butter and sugar until light and fluffy. Add the eggs one at a time, beating thoroughly between each addition.

3 Sift in the flour, then fold in with the lavender, vanilla and milk.

4 Spoon the mixture into the tin and smooth the top level. Bake for about 1 hour, until golden or until a skewer comes out clean when inserted.

5 Leave to cool for 5 minutes before turning out on to a wire rack to go cold.

6 To make the topping, mix the icing sugar with a few drops of water until smooth. Pour over the cake. Decorate with lavender florets.

Nutritional information per portion: Energy 375kcal/1572kJ; Protein 4.7g; Carbohydrate 46.2g, of which sugars 30g; Fat 20.4g, of which saturates 12.1g; Cholesterol 118mg; Calcium 111mg; Fibre 0.7g; Sodium 241mg.

COOK'S TIP
Dried lavender is stronger in flavour than fresh florets, so use half the amount.

Spice cake

Cardamom, cloves and allspice, with the more usual cake spices, give this cake a heady blend that smells good as you take it out of the oven. The flavour will improve after a few days, so make the cake in advance and wrap well. This will keep for up to five days in an airtight container.

SERVES 20

butter, for greasing
breadcrumbs, for sprinkling
500g/1¼lb/5 cups plain
(all-purpose) flour
20ml/4 tsp baking powder
pinch of salt
350g/12oz/1½ cups light muscovado
(brown) sugar
10ml/2 tsp ground cinnamon
1.5ml/¼ tsp ground allspice
1.5ml/¼ tsp ground cloves
2.5ml/½ tsp freshly grated nutmeg
1.5ml/¼ tsp ground cardamom
400–450ml/14–15fl oz/1⅔–2 cups milk

1 Preheat the oven to 150°C/300°F/ Gas 2. Grease a 20–23cm/8–9in round deep cake tin (pan) and sprinkle with breadcrumbs. Remove the excess crumbs.

2 Sift the flour, baking powder and salt into a large bowl. Stir in the sugar, cinnamon, allspice, cloves, nutmeg and cardamom.

3 Gradually add the milk to the mixture, stirring all the time, then whisk until it is smooth and with a pourable consistency.

4 Pour the mixture into the prepared tin and bake for 1½ hours, or until a skewer inserted into the centre comes out clean. Leave to stand in the tin for 5 minutes.

5 Turn out on to a wire rack to go cold. Wrap the cake in foil and store for at least 3 days before eating to allow the flavour of the spices to develop fully.

Nutritional information per portion: Energy 166kcal/ 708kJ; Protein 3.2g; Carbohydrate 39.2g, of which sugars 19.6g; Fat 0.7g, of which saturates 0.3g; Cholesterol 1.2mg; Calcium 80mg; Fibre 0.7g; Sodium 227mg.

Coffee and mint cream cake

Ground almonds give this buttery coffee-flavoured sponge a moist texture and delicate flavour. It is sandwiched together with a generous filling of mint buttercream, which contrasts wonderfully with the coffee. Keep this cake for up to three days in a cool place.

SERVES 8

175g/6oz/³⁄₄ cup unsalted butter, softened, plus extra for greasing
15ml/1 tbsp ground coffee infused (steeped) in 25ml/1¹⁄₂ tbsp near-boiling water for 4 minutes, then strained and cooled
175g/6oz/scant 1 cup caster (superfine) sugar
225g/8oz/2 cups self-raising (self-rising) flour, sifted
50g/2oz/¹⁄₂ cup ground almonds
3 eggs
small sprigs of fresh mint, to decorate

FOR THE FILLING
50g/2oz/¹⁄₄ cup unsalted butter
115g/4oz/1 cup icing (confectioners') sugar, sifted, plus extra for dusting
2 drops of peppermint extract plus 15ml/1 tbsp milk

1 Preheat the oven to 180°C/350°F/Gas 4. Grease and line two 18cm/7in round shallow cake tins (pans).

2 Put the butter, infused ground coffee, sugar, flour, almonds and eggs in a large bowl. Beat well for 1 minute until blended.

3 Divide the mixture evenly between the tins and smooth the top level. Bake for 25 minutes, or until well risen and firm to the touch. Leave in the tins for 5 minutes, then turn out on to a wire rack to go cold.

4 To make the filling, cream the butter, icing sugar, peppermint extract and milk together in a bowl until light and fluffy.

5 Remove the lining paper from the sponges and sandwich together with the filling. Generously dust the top with icing sugar. Top with the fresh mint leaves just before serving.

Nutritional information per portion: Energy 508kcal/2127kJ; Protein 6.5g; Carbohydrate 59.6g, of which sugars 38.5g; Fat 28.8g, of which saturates 16.1g; Cholesterol 136mg; Calcium 148mg; Fibre 1.3g; Sodium 341mg.

Coconut and coffee cake

Some flavours work particularly well together and make natural partners, such as coconut and coffee, and the combination is at its best here. Ground coffee has a good strong flavour that is perfect for this cake. It will keep for up to five days in an airtight container.

SERVES 9

75g/3oz/6 tbsp butter, plus extra
    for greasing
25g/1oz/2 tbsp caster (superfine) sugar
175g/6oz/3/4 cup golden (light
    corn) syrup
40g/11/2oz/1/2 cup desiccated (dry
    unsweetened shredded) coconut
175g/6oz/11/2 cups plain
    (all-purpose) flour
2.5ml/1/2 tsp bicarbonate of soda
    (baking soda)
2 eggs, lightly beaten
45ml/3 tbsp ground coffee infused
    (steeped) in 75ml/5 tbsp
    near-boiling milk for 4 minutes,
    then strained

FOR THE ICING

115g/4oz/1/2 cup butter, softened
225g/8oz/2 cups icing (confectioners')
    sugar, sifted
25g/1oz/1/3 cup shredded or flaked
    coconut, toasted

1 Preheat the oven to 160°C/325°F/Gas 3. Grease and line a 20cm/8in square deep cake tin (pan) with baking parchment.

2 Heat the remaining butter, caster sugar, golden syrup and desiccated coconut in a pan, stirring with a wooden spoon, until completely melted.

3 Sift the flour and bicarbonate of soda into the butter mixture. Add the eggs and 45ml/3 tbsp of the coffee-flavoured milk. Mix well.

4 Spoon the mixture into the prepared tin and smooth it level.

5 Bake for 40–50 minutes, or until well risen and firm.

6 Cool the cake for 10 minutes, then turn out on to a wire rack to go cold. Remove the lining papers.

7 To make the icing, beat the softened butter until smooth, then gradually beat in the icing sugar and remaining coffee-flavoured milk to give a soft consistency.

8 Spread over the top of the cake with a flat-bladed knife and decorate with toasted coconut. Cut into 5cm/2in squares to serve.

Nutritional information per portion: Energy 418kcal/
1756kJ; Protein 3.7g; Carbohydrate 59.7g, of which sugars
44.9g; Fat 20g, of which saturates 13g; Cholesterol
90mg; Calcium 57mg; Fibre 1g; Sodium 225mg.

Pumpkin and banana cake

Rather like a cross between a carrot cake and banana bread, this luscious cake is an excellent way of using some of the scooped-out pumpkin flesh from making Hallowe'en lanterns. A cream cheese topping provides a delicious contrast to the dense moist cake. This is best eaten fresh.

SERVES 12

225g/8oz/2 cups self-raising
   (self-rising) flour
7.5ml/1½ tsp baking powder
2.5ml/½ tsp ground cinnamon
2.5ml/½ tsp ground ginger
130g/4½oz/½ cup soft light
   brown sugar
75g/3oz/¾ cup pecan nuts or
   walnuts, chopped
115g/4oz pumpkin flesh, coarsely grated
2 small ripe bananas, peeled and mashed
2 eggs, lightly beaten
150ml/¼ pint/⅔ cup sunflower oil

FOR THE TOPPING
50g/2oz/¼ cup unsalted butter, at
   room temperature
150g/5oz/⅔ cup soft white
   (farmers') cheese
1.5ml/¼ tsp vanilla extract
115g/4oz/1 cup icing
   (confectioners') sugar
pecan halves, to decorate

1 Preheat the oven to 180°C/350°F/ Gas 4. Line the base and sides of a round deep 20cm/8in cake tin (pan) with baking parchment.

2 Sift the flour, baking powder, cinnamon and ginger into a large bowl to combine. Stir in the sugar, chopped pecan nuts or walnuts and grated pumpkin until thoroughly mixed. Make a slight hollow in the middle of the dry ingredients.

3 In a separate bowl, combine the bananas, eggs and sunflower oil, then stir into the dry ingredients. Spoon into the prepared tin and smooth the top level.

4 Bake for 45–50 minutes, or until a skewer inserted into the centre comes out clean. Cool for 10 minutes, then turn on to a wire rack.

5 To make the topping, beat the butter, soft cheese and vanilla extract in a bowl until smooth. Sift in the icing sugar. Beat until creamy. Spread over the cake and decorate with pecan halves. Chill for 1 hour to allow the topping to harden.

Nutritional information per portion: Energy 388kcal/ 1619kJ; Protein 4.5g; Carbohydrate 40.2g, of which sugars 25.4g; Fat 24.4g, of which saturates 7.8g; Cholesterol 53mg; Calcium 64mg; Fibre 1.1g; Sodium 83mg.

Pecan cake

Ground pecan nuts give this light cake a mellow flavour, which is further enriched with butter and honey drizzled over the cake once cooked. Serve with a spoonful of whipped cream to make an unusual dessert. Keep refrigerated for up to three days.

SERVES 8

115g/4oz/½ cup butter, softened, plus
    extra for greasing
115g/4oz/1 cup pecan nuts
75g/3oz/¾ cup plain (all-purpose) flour
115g/4oz/½ cup soft light brown sugar
5ml/1 tsp vanilla extract
4 large (US extra large) eggs, separated
pinch of salt
12 whole pecan nuts, to decorate
whipped cream, to serve

FOR DRIZZLING

50g/2oz/¼ cup butter
120ml/4fl oz/scant ½ cup clear
    (runny) honey

1 Preheat the oven to 180°C/350°F/ Gas 4. Grease and line a 20cm/8in round shallow cake tin (pan) with baking parchment.

2 Toast the pecan nuts in a frying pan for 5 minutes, shaking often. Grind the nuts in a blender or food processor. Stir in the flour.

3 In a mixing bowl, beat the butter and sugar together until light and fluffy, then beat in the vanilla extract and egg yolks.

4 Put the egg whites and salt into a clean, grease-free bowl and whisk until they form soft peaks.

5 Fold the beaten whites into the butter mixture, then gently fold in the flour and nut mixture.

6 Spoon the batter into the prepared tin and bake for 30 minutes, or until a skewer inserted in the centre comes out clean.

7 Allow the cake to cool in the tin for 5 minutes, then turn out on to a wire rack to go cold. Remove the lining paper.

8 Arrange the pecan nuts in a circle on top of the cake. Transfer to a serving plate. Melt the butter for drizzling in a small pan, add the honey and bring to the boil, stirring.

9 Lower the heat and simmer for 3 minutes. Pour over the cake. Serve with whipped cream.

Nutritional information per portion: Energy 428kcal/ 1785kJ; Protein 6.2g; Carbohydrate 34.7g, of which sugars 27.4g; Fat 30.5g, of which saturates 12.5g; Cholesterol 158mg; Calcium 51mg; Fibre 1g; Sodium 170mg.

Coffee and walnut roll

The classic combination of coffee and walnuts in a cake give it a delicious flavour. This light and fluffy sponge, with its smooth and creamy filling, should be eaten fresh.

SERVES 8

butter, for greasing

3 eggs

75g/3oz/6 tbsp caster (superfine) sugar, plus
   extra for dusting

75g/3oz/³⁄₄ cup self-raising
   (self-rising) flour

10ml/2 tsp ground coffee infused (steeped)
   in 15ml/1 tbsp near-boiling water for 4
   minutes, then strained

50g/2oz/¹⁄₂ cup toasted walnuts,
   finely chopped

FOR THE FILLING

115g/4oz/generous ¹⁄₂ cup caster
   (superfine) sugar, plus extra for dusting

50ml/2fl oz/¹⁄₄ cup cold water

2 egg yolks

115g/4oz/¹⁄₂ cup unsalted butter, softened

15ml/1 tbsp Cointreau or orange liqueur

1 Preheat the oven to 200°C/400°F/Gas 6. Grease and line a 33 x 23cm/ 13 x 9in Swiss roll tin (jelly roll pan) with baking parchment.

2 Whisk the eggs and sugar together in a large bowl until pale and thick. Sift the flour over the mixture and fold in with the coffee and walnuts. Pour into the tin and bake for 10–12 minutes, until golden.

3 Turn the cake out on to a piece of baking parchment sprinkled with caster sugar, peel off the lining paper and cool for about 2 minutes. Trim the edges and roll up from one of the short ends, using the baking parchment to help. Leave to cool, still rolled up in the baking parchment.

4 To make the filling, put the sugar in a pan with the water over a low heat until dissolved. Boil rapidly until the syrup reaches 105°C/220°F on a sugar thermometer. Pour the syrup over the egg yolks, whisking all the time, until thick and mousse-like. Gradually add the butter, then whisk in the orange liqueur. Leave to cool and thicken.

5 Unroll the sponge and spread with filling. Re-roll and place on a serving plate, seam-side down.

6 Dust with extra caster sugar and chill until ready to serve.

Nutritional information per portion: Energy 357kcal/1489kJ; Protein 4.1g; Carbohydrate 31.9g, of which sugars 28.7g; Fat 24.6g, of which saturates 11.9g; Cholesterol 125mg; Calcium 43mg; Fibre 0.4g; Sodium 153mg.

Pear and cardamom spice cake

Fresh pears and cardamom, a classic combination of flavours, are used together in this moist fruit and nut cake that has added crunch from the poppy seeds. It makes a delicious and mouthwatering tea-time treat. This cake keeps in an airtight container for up to five days.

SERVES 8–12

115g/4oz/½ cup butter, plus extra
   for greasing
115g/4oz/generous ½ cup caster
   (superfine) sugar
2 eggs, beaten
225g/8oz/2 cups plain (all-purpose) flour
15ml/1 tbsp baking powder
30ml/2 tbsp milk

crushed seeds from 2 cardamom
   pods
50g/2oz/½ cup walnuts, chopped
15ml/1 tbsp poppy seeds
500g/1¼lb dessert pears, peeled, cored
   and thinly sliced
3 walnut halves
45ml/3 tbsp clear honey

1 Preheat the oven to 180°C/350°F/ Gas 4. Grease and line a 20cm/8in round deep cake tin (pan) with baking parchment.

2 Beat the butter and sugar until pale and light. Beat in the eggs a little at a time. Sift the flour and baking powder over the butter and sugar mixture; fold in with the milk.

3 Add the cardamom seeds, chopped nuts and poppy seeds. Reserve one-third of the pear slices, and chop the remainder. Fold in the chopped pears.

4 Transfer the batter to the tin and smooth the top, making a small dip in the centre. Put the walnut halves in the centre and fan the pear slices around them, overlapping each slice and covering the batter. Bake for 1¼–1½ hours, or until a skewer inserted comes out clean.

5 Cool the cake in the tin for 20 minutes, turn out then transfer to a wire rack. Remove the lining paper. While the cake is warm, brush the top with honey. Leave to go cold.

Nutritional information per portion: Energy 231kcal/ 970kJ; Protein 3.7g; Carbohydrate 29g, of which sugars 14.7g; Fat 12g, of which saturates 5.5g; Cholesterol 52.3mg; Calcium 49mg; Fibre 1.6g; Sodium 73.5mg.

Pineapple and ginger upside-down cake

This light and moist cake has a sticky ginger glaze over stem ginger and pineapple pieces, which are arranged in the cake tin before the cake batter is added. It is superb served warm as a dessert with home-made custard or thick cream. This cake will keep refrigerated, for two days.

SERVES 8

20g/3/4oz/1½ tbsp butter, plus extra
    for greasing
2 pieces preserved stem ginger, chopped,
    plus 60ml/4 tbsp syrup
450g/1lb can pineapple pieces in natural
    juice, drained
250g/9oz/2¼ cups wholemeal (whole-
    wheat) self-raising (self-rising) flour
15ml/1 tbsp baking powder
5ml/1 tsp ground ginger
5ml/1 tsp ground cinnamon
115g/4oz/½ cup soft light brown sugar
250ml/8fl oz/1 cup milk
45ml/3 tbsp sunflower oil
1 banana, peeled

1 Preheat the oven to 180°C/235°F/ Gas 4. Grease and line a 20cm/8in round deep cake tin (pan).

2 Melt the butter in a small pan over a gentle heat, then stir in the ginger syrup. Turn up the heat until the liquid thickens.

3 Pour the mixture into the prepared tin and smooth out to the sides.

4 Arrange the stem ginger, and one-third of the pineapple pieces, in the syrup in the bottom of the cake tin. Set aside.

5 Sift together the flour, baking powder and spices into a large bowl, then stir in the sugar.

6 In a food processor or blender, blend the milk, oil, the remaining pineapple and the banana until almost smooth, then add this mixture to the flour. Stir until mixed.

7 Spoon the mixture over the pineapple and ginger pieces in the tin and smooth level.

8 Bake for 45 minutes, or until a skewer inserted into the centre of the cake comes out clean. Leave to cool slightly, then place a serving plate over the tin and turn upside down. Remove the lining paper.

Nutritional information per portion: Energy 358kcal/ 1508kJ; Protein 4.6g; Carbohydrate 55.2g, of which sugars 47.1g; Fat 14.8g, of which saturates 8.3g; Cholesterol 126mg; Calcium 63mg; Fibre 1g; Sodium 126mg.

Semolina cake with poppy seeds

A combination of poppy seeds, vanilla and semolina is used for this delicious cake. Poppy seeds add texture and extra flavour and the lemon syrup adds a delightful tanginess.

SERVES 6–8

115g/4oz/¹/₂ cup butter

175g/6oz/scant 1 cup sugar

30–45ml/2–3 tbsp white poppy seeds

5–10ml/1–2 tsp vanilla extract

2 eggs

450g/1lb/2²/₃ cups fine semolina

5ml/1 tsp baking powder

2.5ml/¹/₂ tsp bicarbonate of soda
   (baking soda)

175g/6fl oz/³/₄ cup strained yogurt

16 blanched almonds, halved

FOR THE SYRUP

250g/8fl oz/1 cup water

450g/1lb/2¹/₄ cups sugar

juice of 1 lemon

1 First make the syrup. Boil the water with the sugar, stirring constantly, until dissolved. Stir in the lemon juice, reduce the heat and simmer for 10–15 minutes, until the syrup coats the back of a wooden spoon. Leave the syrup to cool.

2 Preheat the oven to 180°C/350°F/Gas 4 and grease a 20 x 30cm/8 x 12in baking tin (pan). Cream the butter with the sugar, beat in the poppy seeds and vanilla and add the eggs one at a time. Sift the semolina with the baking powder and bicarbonate of soda and fold it into the creamed mixture with the yogurt.

3 Turn the mixture into the prepared tin, spreading it evenly to the edges. Place the almonds on top, arranged in lines, and bake for about 30 minutes, or until a skewer inserted comes out clean. Pour the syrup over the hot cake. Cut the cake into diamonds and return to the oven for 5 minutes to create a sticky top.

Nutritional information per portion: Energy 664kcal/2809kJ; Protein 9.9g; Carbohydrate 127g, of which sugars 83.4g; Fat 16.5g, of which saturates 8.5g; Cholesterol 81mg; Calcium 120mg; Fibre 1.5g; Sodium 156mg.

Yogurt cake with pistachio nuts

Flavoured with vanilla and pistachios, this unusual cake contains very little flour. The texture is lightened with whisked egg whites. Serve with fresh fruit and eat the same day.

SERVES 8–12

butter, for greasing

3 eggs, separated

75g/3oz/scant ½ cup caster
   (superfine) sugar

seeds from 2 vanilla pods (beans)

300ml/½ pint/1¼ cup Greek (US
   strained plain) yogurt

grated rind and juice of 1 lemon

15ml/1 tbsp plain (all-purpose) flour

handful of pistachio nuts,
   roughly chopped

90ml/6 tbsp crème fraîche, to serve

4–6 fresh passion fruit, or 50g/2oz/½
   cup summer berries, to serve

1 Preheat the oven to 180°C/350°F/Gas 4. Grease and line a 25cm/10in square shallow tin (pan) with baking parchment.

2 In a mixing bowl, beat the egg yolks with 50g/2oz/¼ cup sugar until pale and fluffy. Beat in the vanilla seeds and stir in the yogurt, lemon rind and juice. Sift in the flour and beat well until light and airy.

3 Put the egg whites into a clean, grease-free bowl and whisk until they form stiff peaks, then gradually whisk in the rest of the sugar to form soft peaks. Fold the whisked whites into the yogurt mixture. Turn into the cake tin.

4 Put the tin in a roasting pan and pour water in the pan to come halfway up the cake tin. Bake for 20 minutes, or until risen and just set. Sprinkle the nuts over the cake and bake for another 20 minutes. Serve warm or cold with crème fraîche and a spoonful of fruit.

Nutritional information per portion: Energy 152kcal/638kJ; Protein 6.6g; Carbohydrate 16g, of which sugars 14.1g; Fat 7.9g, of which saturates 3.4g; Cholesterol 95mg; Calcium 99mg; Fibre 0.1g; Sodium 71mg.

Moist orange and almond cake

There are many techniques for adding moisture and flavour to cake batters. Here a whole orange is cooked slowly until completely tender and then blended to a purée. Ground almonds add richness and moisture. Eat fresh, served with orange slices and whipped cream.

SERVES 8

1 large orange, washed
butter, for greasing
3 eggs
225g/8oz/generous 1 cup caster
    (superfine) sugar
5ml/1 tsp baking powder
25g/1oz/¼ cup plain (all-purpose) flour
225g/8oz/2 cups ground almonds
icing (confectioners') sugar, for dusting
whipped cream and orange slices
    (optional), to serve

1 Pierce the orange with a skewer. Put it in a deep pan and cover with water. Bring to the boil, lower the heat, cover and simmer for 1 hour, until soft. Drain, then cool.

2 Preheat the oven to 180°C/350°F/ Gas 4. Grease and line a 20cm/8in round deep cake tin (pan).

3 Cut the orange in half and discard the pips. Put the orange, skin and all, in a blender or food processor and purée until smooth and pulpy.

4 In a bowl, whisk the eggs and sugar. Fold in the baking powder, flour and almonds, then the purée.

5 Pour into the prepared tin, level the surface and bake for 1 hour, or until a skewer inserted into the middle comes out clean.

6 Allow to cool for 10 minutes, then turn out on to a wire rack to go cold. Peel off the lining paper.

7 Dust the cake with icing sugar and serve with whipped cream. Tuck thick orange slices under the cake just before serving, if you like.

COOK'S TIP
Do not use a microwave to cook the orange.

Nutritional information per portion: Energy 187kcal/ 783kJ; Protein 5.1g; Carbohydrate 20g, of which sugars 18.2g; Fat 10.2g, of which saturates 1.1g; Cholesterol 41mg; Calcium 60mg; Fibre 1.4g; Sodium 19mg.

Apple and cinnamon cake

Dates and grated apples bring lots of fruitiness and moisture to this spicy cake mix, which also includes gram flour (made from ground chickpeas) and coconut milk, giving it an Asian touch. Good for packed lunches, this cake will keep for up to five days in an airtight container.

SERVES 8–10

115g/4oz/½ cup butter, plus extra
    for greasing
200g/7oz/generous 1 cup dried, stoned
    (pitted) dates
1–2 tart eating apples or 1 cooking apple,
    about 225g/8oz
12.5ml/2½ tsp mixed (apple
    pie) spice
pinch of salt
150g/5oz/1¼ cups wholemeal (whole-
    wheat) flour
115g/4oz/1 cup gram flour
10ml/2 tsp baking powder
75g/3oz/generous ½ cup raisins
2 eggs, beaten
175ml/6fl oz/¾ cup unsweetened
    coconut milk

1 Preheat the oven to 180°C/350°F/ Gas 4. Grease and line a 20cm/8in deep square cake tin (pan) with baking parchment.

2 Combine the butter and dates in a food processor.

3 Peel, core and grate the apple and add to the butter and date mixture with the mixed spice and salt. Process until thoroughly blended.

4 Spoon the mixture into a bowl. In batches, sift and fold in the flours and baking powder, alternating with the raisins, beaten eggs and coconut milk.

5 Transfer the mixture to the prepared tin and smooth the top level with a spoon.

6 Bake for 30–40 minutes, or until dark golden and firm, and a skewer inserted comes out clean.

7 Allow the cake to cool in the tin for about 15 minutes before turning it out on to a wire rack to go completely cold.

8 Peel off the lining paper. Slice and serve.

Nutritional information per portion: Energy 587kcal/ 2472kJ; Protein 5.5g; Carbohydrate 92g, of which sugars 69.7g; Fat 24.5g, of which saturates 10.6g; Cholesterol 40mg; Calcium 95mg; Fibre 2.5g; Sodium 129mg.

Almond cake

Toasted almonds are the main ingredient in this light cake, giving it a nutty flavour and an excellent texture. It is best served warm, and a scoop of vanilla or good-quality chocolate ice cream would also go well with it. Eat this fresh, or keep it for one day in an airtight container.

SERVES 4–6

25g/1oz/2 tbsp butter, plus extra
   for greasing
225/8oz/2 cups blanched whole almonds
75g/3oz/¾ cup icing (confectioners')
   sugar, plus extra for dusting
3 eggs
2.5ml/½ tsp almond extract
25g/1oz/¼ cup plain (all-purpose) flour
3 egg whites
15ml/1 tbsp caster (superfine) sugar

1 Preheat the oven to 160°C/325°F/ Gas 3. Grease and line a 23cm/9in round shallow cake tin (pan) with baking parchment.

2 Spread the almonds in an even layer in a baking tray and bake for 10 minutes. Allow the almonds to cool. Set aside a few of the almonds for decoration. Chop the rest, then grind them with half of the icing sugar in a food processor. Transfer to a large bowl.

3 Increase the oven temperature to 200°C/400°F/Gas 6.

4 Add the whole eggs and the remaining icing sugar to the bowl. With an electric whisk, beat until the mixture forms a trail when the beaters are lifted away.

5 In a small pan, melt the butter, then mix into the nut and egg mixture with the almond extract.

6 Sift over the flour and fold in.

7 Whisk the egg whites into a clean, grease-free bowl until they form soft peaks. Add the sugar. Beat until they form stiff peaks.

8 Fold the egg whites into the batter. Spoon into the cake tin. Bake for 15–20 minutes, until golden. Turn out of the tin. Remove the lining papers.

9 Decorate with the toasted almonds and dust with icing sugar.

Nutritional information per portion: Energy 376kcal/ 1568kJ; Protein 13g; Carbohydrate 21.5g, of which sugars 17.3g; Fat 27.2g, of which saturates 4.6g; Cholesterol 104mg; Calcium 120mg; Fibre 2.9g; Sodium 97mg.

Walnut cake

Brandy, orange and cinnamon warmed in a sugar syrup are poured over this baked walnut cake, making it superbly moist and full of complementary flavours. This technique is an excellent way to add flavour and freshness to a cake. Keep this cake, refrigerated, for three days.

SERVES 10–12

150g/5oz/10 tbsp unsalted butter, plus
    extra for greasing
115g/4oz/generous ¹/₂ cup caster
    (superfine) sugar
4 eggs, separated
60ml/4 tbsp brandy
2.5ml/¹/₂ tsp ground cinnamon
300g/11oz/2³/₄ cups walnuts
150g/5oz/1¹/₄ cups self-raising (self-
    rising) flour
5ml/1 tsp baking powder
pinch of salt

FOR THE SYRUP

250g/9oz/1¹/₄ cups caster
    (superfine) sugar
30ml/2 tbsp brandy
2 or 3 strips of pared orange rind
2 cinnamon sticks

1 Preheat the oven to 190°C/375°F/ Gas 5. Grease and line a 35 × 23cm/ 14 × 9in shallow cake tin (pan).

2 In a bowl, beat the butter and sugar together until light and fluffy. Beat in the egg yolks one at a time. Stir in the brandy and cinnamon.

3 Coarsely chop the walnuts, using a food processor, and stir them in.

4 Sift the flour with the baking powder and set aside.

5 Put the egg whites and salt into a clean, grease-free bowl and whisk until they form stiff peaks.

6 Fold the egg whites into the butter and sugar mixture, alternating with tablespoons of flour.

7 Spread the batter evenly in the prepared tin. Bake for about 40 minutes, or until the top is golden and a skewer inserted into the centre comes out clean. Set on a wire rack in the tin.

8 To make the syrup, mix the sugar and 300ml/¹/₂ pint/1¹/₄ cups water in a pan. Heat gently, stirring, until the sugar has dissolved. Bring to the boil, lower the heat and add the brandy, orange rind and cinnamon sticks. Simmer for 10 minutes.

9 Remove the lining paper. Slice the cake into diamonds while still hot and strain the syrup over it. Let it stand for 10–20 minutes, then turn out on to a wire rack to go cold.

Nutritional information per portion: Energy 563kcal/ 2349kJ; Protein 8.5g, Carbohydrate 50.6g, of which sugars 39.2g; Fat 35.3g, of which saturates 10.1g; Cholesterol 108mg; Calcium 114mg; Fibre 1.5g; Sodium 177mg.

Pine nut and almond cake

This unusual recipe uses olive oil, toasted semolina and nuts to give the cake a rich flavour and a dense, grainy texture. It is also very moist because it is soaked in a cinnamon and sugar syrup. Unlike traditional cakes it is not baked in the oven, but heated in a pan. Eat fresh.

SERVES 6–8

500g/1¼lb/2¾ cups caster
   (superfine) sugar
1 cinnamon stick
250ml/8fl oz/1 cup olive oil
350g/12oz/2 cups coarse semolina
50g/2oz/½ cup blanched almonds
30ml/2 tbsp pine nuts
5ml/1 tsp ground cinnamon

1 Put the sugar in a heavy pan with 1 litre/1¾ pints/4 cups cold water and the cinnamon stick. Bring to the boil, stirring until the sugar dissolves, then boil without stirring for 4 minutes to make a syrup.

2 Meanwhile, heat the oil in a separate, heavy pan. When it is almost smoking, add the semolina gradually and stir constantly until it turns light brown.

3 Lower the heat, add the almonds and pine nuts, and brown together for 2–3 minutes, stirring constantly.

4 Take the semolina mixture off the heat and set aside. Remove the cinnamon stick from the hot syrup using a slotted spoon and discard it.

5 Carefully add the hot syrup to the semolina mixture, stirring all the time. The mixture will spit at this point, so stand well away from it.

6 Return the pan to a gentle heat and stir until the syrup has been absorbed and the mixture is smooth.

7 Remove the pan from the heat, cover it with a clean dish towel and leave it to stand for 10 minutes so that any remaining moisture is absorbed.

8 Spoon the mixture into a 20–23cm/8–9in round non-stick cake tin (pan), and set it aside. When cold, unmould it on to a platter and dust it all over with the cinnamon.

Nutritional information per portion: Energy 643kcal/ 2706kJ; Protein 6.8g; Carbohydrate 99.8g, of which sugars 65.7g; Fat 26.8g, of which saturates 3.3g; Cholesterol 0mg; Calcium 56mg; Fibre 1.5g; Sodium 10mg.

Date and walnut spice cake

This deliciously moist and rich spiced cake is topped with a sticky honey and orange glaze. Serve it as a dessert with a generous spoonful of natural yogurt, or crème fraîche, flavoured with grated orange rind. Keep this cake, refrigerated, for up to three days.

SERVES 8

115g/4oz/½ cup unsalted butter, plus
    extra for greasing
175g/6oz/¾ cup soft dark brown sugar
2 eggs
175g/6oz/1½ cups self-raising (self-
    rising) flour, plus extra for dusting
5ml/1 tsp bicarbonate of soda
    (baking soda)
2.5ml/½ tsp freshly grated nutmeg
5ml/1 tsp mixed spice
pinch of salt
175ml/6fl oz/¾ cup buttermilk
50g/2oz/⅓ cup ready-to-eat stoned
    (pitted) dates, chopped
25g/1oz/¼ cup walnuts, chopped

FOR THE TOPPING

60ml/4 tbsp clear honey
45ml/3 tbsp fresh orange juice
15ml/1 tbsp coarsely grated orange rind

1 Preheat the oven to
180°C/350°F/Gas 4. Grease and
lightly flour a 23cm/9in round
deep cake tin (pan).

2 In a bowl, beat the butter and
sugar until light and fluffy,
then beat in the eggs one
at a time.

3 Sift together the flour,
bicarbonate of soda, spices
and salt into a bowl.

4 Add the flour mixture to the egg
and sugar mixture, alternating with
the buttermilk, and mix well. Mix in
the dates and walnuts.

5 Spoon the batter into the cake tin
and smooth the top level.

6 Bake for 50 minutes, or until a
skewer inserted into the centre
comes out clean. Leave to cool for 5
minutes. Turn out on to a wire rack
to go cold.

7 To make the topping, heat the
honey, orange juice and rind in a
pan. Bring to the boil. Boil rapidly,
without stirring, for 3 minutes, or
until syrupy.

8 Prick holes in the top of the cake
and pour over the hot syrup.

Nutritional information per portion: Energy 350kcal/
1472kJ; Protein 5.1g; Carbohydrate 50.3g, of which sugars
34.1g; Fat 15.7g, of which saturates 8.1g; Cholesterol
79mg; Calcium 131mg; Fibre 1g; Sodium 196mg.

Chocolate Cakes

Universally appealing, chocolate is an incredibly versatile ingredient in baking: Chocolate Potato Cake and Chocolate and Beetroot Layer Cake are just a couple of the surprising combinations here. However popular classics such as Death by Chocolate, Devilish Chocolate Roulade, Devil's Food Cake and Black Forest Gateau are also included. Most of these delightful cakes can be kept for around three days, if they last that long!

Simple chocolate cake

Make this easy, everyday chocolate cake and fill it with chocolate buttercream for a sweet afternoon treat that will be popular with all the family. Use a good quality chocolate with more than 70 per cent cocoa solids for the best flavour. Store this cake for up to three days.

SERVES 6–8

150g/5oz/10 tbsp unsalted butter, softened, plus extra for greasing

115g/4oz plain (semisweet) chocolate, broken into pieces

45ml/3 tbsp milk

150g/5oz/generous ½ cup light muscovado (brown) sugar

3 eggs

200g/7oz/1¾ cups self-raising (self-rising) flour

15ml/1 tbsp unsweetened cocoa powder

FOR THE BUTTERCREAM

75g/3oz/6 tbsp unsalted butter, softened

175g/6oz/1½ cups icing (confectioners') sugar, plus extra for dusting

15ml/1 tbsp unsweetened cocoa powder, plus extra for dusting

2.5ml/½ tsp vanilla extract

1 Preheat the oven to 180°C/350°F/ Gas 4. Grease and line two 18cm/ 7in round shallow cake tins (pans).

2 Melt the chocolate with the milk in a heatproof bowl set over a pan of simmering water. Cool.

3 In a bowl, beat the butter with the sugar until fluffy, then beat in the eggs. Stir in the chocolate mixture.

4 Sift the flour and cocoa over the mixture and fold in until evenly mixed. Spoon into the tins and smooth level. Bake for 35–40 minutes, or until risen and firm. Turn out on to wire racks to cool. Remove the lining papers.

5 To make the buttercream, put all the ingredients into a large bowl. Beat well to reach a smooth, spreadable consistency. Sandwich the cake layers together with the buttercream. Dust with cocoa and icing sugar.

Nutritional information per portion: Energy 427kcal/ 1776kJ; Protein 6.1g; Carbohydrate 29.2g, of which sugars 9.8g; Fat 32.6g, of which saturates 19.6g; Cholesterol 139mg; Calcium 65mg; Fibre 1.4g; Sodium 238mg.

Mississippi mud cake

This rich chocolate cake is a variation of Mississippi mud pie, a sticky dessert baked in a pie shell. The cake tastes good served, as you would serve the pie, with a scoop of vanilla ice cream or some whipped cream – or even both. This cake will keep refrigerated for two days.

SERVES 8–10

225g/8oz/1 cup butter, plus extra
    for greasing
unsweetened cocoa powder, for dusting
150g/5oz plain (semisweet) chocolate,
    broken into pieces
300ml/½ pint/1¼ cups strong,
    brewed coffee
50ml/2fl oz/¼ cup bourbon
400g/14oz/2 cups caster
    (superfine) sugar
225g/8oz/2 cups plain (all-purpose) flour
5ml/1 tsp baking powder
2 eggs
7.5ml/1½ tsp vanilla extract

1 Preheat the oven to 140°C/ 275°F/Gas 1. Grease a 25cm/10in round deep cake tin (pan), then dust it lightly with the cocoa powder.

2 Put the chocolate in a heatproof bowl with the coffee, bourbon and butter. Set the bowl over a pan of gently simmering water. Stir the mixture with a wooden spoon until melted and smooth. Remove the bowl from the heat and set aside to cool slightly.

3 Using an electric whisk on low speed, gradually beat the sugar into the chocolate. Continue beating until the sugar dissolves.

4 Increase the speed to medium and add the flour and baking powder. Mix well, then beat in the eggs and vanilla extract.

5 Pour the batter into the tin. Bake for 1 hour 20 minutes, or until a skewer inserted into the centre comes out clean.

6 Cool in the tin for 15 minutes, then turn out on to a wire rack.

7 Place on a serving plate and dust the cake with cocoa powder.

Nutritional information per portion: Energy 534kcal/ 2227kJ; Protein 6.3g; Carbohydrate 49.5g, of which sugars 38.5g; Fat 35.2g, of which saturates 19.6g; Cholesterol 87mg; Calcium 110mg; Fibre 2.1g; Sodium 142mg.

Chocolate sandwich cake

A light chocolate sponge cake is filled and topped with a rich, chocolatey frosting. It makes a good celebration cake, topped with small squares of fudge and white chocolate buttons.

SERVES 10–12

130g/4¹⁄₂oz/generous ¹⁄₂ cup butter, softened, plus extra for greasing
250g/9oz/1¹⁄₄ cups caster (superfine) sugar
3 eggs, beaten
225g/8oz/2 cups plain (all-purpose) flour
5ml/1 tsp bicarbonate of soda (baking soda)
50g/2oz/¹⁄₂ cup unsweetened cocoa power
250ml/8fl oz/1 cup buttermilk

FOR THE CHOCOLATE BUTTERCREAM

50g/2oz dark (bittersweet) chocolate
175g/6oz/1¹⁄₂ cups icing (confectioners') sugar, sifted
115g/4oz/¹⁄₂ cup unsalted butter, softened
few drops of vanilla extract

1 Preheat the oven to 180°C/350°F/ Gas 4. Grease and line two 20cm/8in round shallow cake tins (pans) with baking parchment.

2 Cream the butter and sugar until light and fluffy. Gradually beat in the eggs. Beat in the flour, bicarbonate of soda and cocoa in batches. Add the buttermilk and mix well.

3 Spoon into the prepared tins and bake for 30–35 minutes, or until firm to the touch. Let stand for 5 minutes, then turn out of the tins, peel off the papers and leave on a wire rack to go cold.

4 To make the buttercream, melt the chocolate in a heatproof bowl set over a pan of gently simmering water. Stir occasionally. Allow to cool slightly.

5 In another bowl, beat the icing sugar with the butter until soft and creamy. Mix in the melted chocolate.

6 Use half of the buttercream to sandwich the cakes together, and spread the remainder on the top of the cake. Store in the refrigerator.

Nutritional information per portion: Energy 430kcal/ 1790kJ; Protein 7.8g; Carbohydrate 29.5g, of which sugars 28.8g; Fat 32.1g, of which saturates 13.6g; Cholesterol 96mg; Calcium 92mg; Fibre 1.9g; Sodium 125mg.

Chocolate, almond and coffee cake

This easy all-in-one cake recipe is quick to make. Add a lovely coffee buttercream for the filling and topping, and the chocolate cake is transformed into something extra special.

SERVES 8

175g/6oz/¾ cup butter, softened, plus
    extra for greasing
175g/6oz/1½ cups self-raising (self-
    rising) flour
25ml/1½ tbsp unsweetened
    cocoa powder
pinch of salt
175g/6oz/¾ cup soft dark brown sugar
50g/2oz/½ cup ground almonds
3 large (US extra large) eggs,
    lightly beaten

**FOR THE COFFEE
BUTTERCREAM**
175g/6oz/¾ cup unsalted butter
350g/12oz/3 cups icing (confectioners')
    sugar, sifted
30ml/2 tbsp coffee extract
whole hazelnuts or pecan nuts, to
    decorate (optional)

1 Preheat the oven to 180°C/350°F/
Gas 4. Grease and line two
18cm/7in round shallow cake
tins (pans).

2 Sift the flour, cocoa and salt into a
large bowl.

3 In another bowl, cream the butter
with the sugar until light and fluffy.

4 Add the ground almonds, eggs,
flour and cocoa, and beat well.
Divide the batter between the tins.

5 Bake for 25–30 minutes. Turn out
on a wire rack to go cold. Remove
the paper lining.

6 To make the buttercream, beat the
butter, then gradually beat in the
icing sugar and coffee extract.

7 Put around one quarter of
the buttercream into a small
piping (pastry) bag fitted with
a star nozzle.

8 Sandwich the cakes together
with some of the buttercream.
Cover the top and sides with the
remaining mixture.

9 Pipe rosettes around the top of
the cake and decorate with whole
hazelnuts or pecan nuts, if you like.

Nutritional information per portion: Energy 737kcal/
3085kJ; Protein 7g; Carbohydrate 86.4g, of which sugars
69.6g; Fat 43g, of which saturates 24g; Cholesterol
1.4mg; Calcium 1.06mg; Fibre 12.2g; Sodium 3.28mg.

Frosted chocolate fudge cake

Rich and dreamy, this chocolate cake has added depth of flavour from muscovado sugar and thick yogurt. The chocolate fudge frosting also contains yogurt, giving it a creamy consistency. It couldn't be easier to make, or more delicious to eat. Keep, refrigerated, for up to three days.

SERVES 8

175g/6oz/³/₄ cup unsalted butter, softened, plus extra for greasing

115g/4oz plain (semisweet) chocolate, broken into pieces

200g/7oz/scant 1 cup light muscovado (brown) sugar

5ml/1 tsp vanilla extract

3 eggs, beaten

150ml/¹/₄ pint/²/₃ cup Greek (US strained plain) yogurt

150g/5oz/1¹/₄ cups self-raising (self-rising) flour

FOR THE FROSTING AND CHOCOLATE CURLS

2255g/8oz plain (semisweet) chocolate, broken into pieces

50g/2oz/¹/₄ cup unsalted butter

90ml/6 tbsp Greek (US strained plain) yogurt

350g/12oz/3 cups icing (confectioners') sugar, plus extra for dusting

1 Preheat the oven to 190°C/375°F/Gas 5. Grease and line two 20cm/8in round shallow cake tins (pans) with baking parchment.

2 Melt the chocolate in a heatproof bowl over a pan of simmering water.

3 Meanwhile, in a large bowl, beat the butter with the sugar until light and fluffy. Beat in the vanilla extract, then gradually beat in the egg in small quantities, beating well after each addition.

4 Stir in the melted chocolate and yogurt. Sift the flour over the mixture, then fold in gently with a large metal spoon.

5 Divide the mixture between the tins. Bake for 25–30 minutes, or until the cakes are firm to the touch. Leave to stand for 5 minutes, then turn out on to a wire rack to go cold. Remove the lining papers.

6 To make the chocolate curls, melt 115g/4oz of the chocolate in a heatproof bowl set over a pan of gently simmering water.

7 Spread the melted chocolate on to a clean, cold hard surface, preferably marble, and allow to set.

8 Meanwhile, to make the frosting, melt the rest of the chocolate and all the butter in a medium pan over a gentle heat.

9 Stir in the yogurt and icing sugar. Mix with a rubber spatula until smooth, then beat until the frosting begins to cool and thicken slightly.

10 Use a third of the mixture to sandwich the cakes together. Working quickly, spread the rest of the frosting over the top and sides.

11 To make the curls, using a long, sharp knife, scrape along the surface of the set chocolate to make thin curled shavings.

12 Position the shavings on the cake and then dust with icing sugar.

Nutritional information per portion: Energy 753kcal/3160kJ; Protein 8g; Carbohydrate 105.4g, of which sugars 90.9g; Fat 36.6g, of which saturates 21.7g; Cholesterol 133mg; Calcium 133mg; Fibre 1.3g; Sodium 224mg.

Devilish chocolate roulade

This luxurious roulade can be made a day ahead and then filled and rolled before serving. It has a rich brandy, chocolate and mascarpone filling and is decorated with chocolate-dipped strawberries to make it extra special. Once filled, keep it, refrigerated, for up to two days.

SERVES 6–8

butter, for greasing
175g/6oz plain (semisweet) chocolate,
    broken into pieces
4 eggs, separated
115g/4oz/generous ½ cup caster
    (superfine) sugar
unsweetened cocoa powder, for dusting

FOR THE FILLING

225g/8oz plain (semisweet) chocolate,
    broken into pieces
45ml/3 tbsp brandy
2 eggs, separated
250g/9oz/generous 1 cup mascarpone
chocolate-dipped strawberries

1 Preheat the oven to 180°C/350°F/Gas 4. Grease and line a 33 × 23cm/ 13 × 9in Swiss roll tin (jelly roll pan) with baking parchment.

2 Melt the chocolate in a heatproof bowl over a pan of gently simmering water, then remove from the heat.

3 Whisk the egg yolks and sugar in a bowl until pale and thick, then stir in the melted chocolate.

4 Put the egg whites into a clean, grease-free bowl and whisk until they form soft peaks, then fold lightly and evenly into the egg and chocolate mixture.

5 Pour the mixture into the prepared tin and smooth level. Bake for 15–20 minutes, or until well risen and firm to the touch. Dust a sheet of baking parchment with cocoa. Turn the sponge out on to the paper, cover with a clean dish towel and leave to cool.

6 To make the filling, melt the chocolate with the brandy in a heatproof bowl set over a pan of gently simmering water. Remove from the heat.

7 Beat the egg yolks together, then beat into the warm chocolate mixture until smooth.

8 Put the egg whites into a clean, grease-free bowl and whisk until they form soft peaks. Fold them lightly and evenly into the filling in three batches until the mixture is light and smooth. Cool completely.

9 Uncover the roulade, remove the lining paper and spread with most of the mascarpone. Spread the chocolate mixture over the top, then roll up from a long side to enclose the filling.

10 Transfer to a serving plate, top with mascarpone, fresh chocolate-dipped strawberries, and dust with cocoa powder.

CHOCOLATE-DIPPED STRAWBERRIES
Rinse and dry the strawberries with kitchen paper. Holding the stem or the leaves, dip the lower half of each strawberry into some good quality melted chocolate. Leave to set on a baking sheet lined with baking parchment.

Nutritional information per portion: Energy 486kcal/2022kJ; Protein 10.2g; Carbohydrate 32.8g, of which sugars 32.4g; Fat 34.5g, of which saturates 19.9g; Cholesterol 189mg; Calcium 41mg; Fibre 1.3g; Sodium 143mg.

Black Forest gateau

Perhaps the most famous chocolate cake of all, this Kirsch-flavoured gateau is layered with fresh cream containing chopped black cherries, and is decorated with cherries and chocolate curls.

SERVES 10–12

75g/3oz/6 tbsp butter, melted, plus extra
   for greasing
5 eggs
175g/6oz/scant 1 cup caster
   (superfine) sugar
50g/2oz/$^{1}/_{2}$ cup plain (all-purpose)
   flour, sifted
50g/2oz/$^{1}/_{2}$ cup unsweetened cocoa
   powder, sifted

FOR THE FILLING AND TOPPING
75–90ml/5–6 tbsp Kirsch
600ml/1 pint/2$^{1}/_{2}$ cups double
   (heavy) cream
425g/15oz can black cherries, drained, pitted
   and chopped

FOR THE DECORATION
225g/8oz plain (semisweet) chocolate, to
   make chocolate curls, see pages 82–83
15–20 fresh cherries, preferably with stems
sifted icing (confectioners') sugar (optional)

1 Preheat the oven to 180°C/350°F/Gas 4. Grease and line two 20cm/8in round deep cake tins (pans) with baking parchment.

2 Beat the eggs and sugar with an electric whisk for about 10 minutes, or until the mixture is thick and pale.

3 Sift together the flour and cocoa powder, then sift again into the whisked mixture. Fold in gently using a metal spoon and a figure-of-eight motion. Slowly trickle in the cooled melted butter and fold in gently.

4 Divide the batter between the tins and smooth level. Bake for 30 minutes, until springy to the touch. Leave in the tins for 5 minutes, then turn on to a wire rack to cool. Peel off the lining papers. Cut each cake in half horizontally. Sprinkle the four layers evenly with the Kirsch.

5 In a large bowl, whip the cream until it holds soft peaks. Transfer two-thirds of the cream to another bowl and stir in the chopped cherries. Spread a layer of cake with one-third of the filling. Top with another cake layer and continue, finishing with the cake top. With the remaining cream, cover the top and sides of the gateau. Decorate with chocolate curls, cherries and icing sugar.

Nutritional information per portion: Energy Energy 448kcal/1864kJ; Protein 4.8g; Carbohydrate 26.4g, of which sugars 22.7g; Fat 35.2g, of which saturates 21.1g; Cholesterol 161mg; Calcium 61.8mg; Fibre 0.8g; Sodium 121mg.

Death by chocolate

This rich chocolate confection has layers of jam and brandy-flavoured chocolate filling between layers of light cake. It is covered with chocolate ganache – a rich chocolate-truffle topping.

SERVES 16–20

115g/4oz/¹⁄₂ cup unsalted butter, plus extra
    for greasing
225g/8oz plain (semisweet) chocolate,
    broken into pieces
150ml/¹⁄₄ pint/²⁄₃ cup milk
225g/8oz/1 cup light muscovado
    (brown) sugar
10ml/2 tsp vanilla extract
2 eggs, separated
150ml/¹⁄₄ pint/²⁄₃ cup sour cream
225g/8oz/2 cups self-raising
    (self-rising) flour
5ml/1 tsp baking powder

FOR THE FILLING

60ml/4 tbsp seedless raspberry jam
60ml/4 tbsp brandy
400g/14oz plain (semisweet) chocolate,
    broken into pieces
200g/7oz/scant 1 cup unsalted butter
plain and white chocolate curls, and
    chocolate-dipped physalis, to decorate

FOR THE GANACHE

250ml/8fl oz/1 cup double (heavy) cream
225g/8oz plain (semisweet) chocolate,
    broken into pieces

1 Preheat the oven to 180°C/350°F/Gas 4. Grease and line a 23cm/9in round deep cake tin (pan) with baking parchment.

2 Put the chocolate, butter and milk in a pan. Stir over a very low heat until the chocolate melts. Remove from the heat. Beat in the sugar and vanilla.

3 Beat the egg yolks and cream, then beat into the chocolate mixture. Sift the flour and baking powder over the mixture and fold in. Whisk the egg whites until stiff, then fold into the mixture. Spoon into the cake tin and bake for 45–55 minutes. Turn on to a wire rack to go cold. Remove the lining papers. Slice into three even layers.

4 To make the filling, warm the jam with 15ml/1 tbsp of the brandy in a small pan. Brush over one side of two cake layers, then leave to set. Put the remaining brandy in the pan with the chocolate and butter. Melt gently over a low heat, stirring until smooth. Cool until the filling is just beginning to thicken. Spread one layer of the cake with half of the chocolate filling. Top with a second layer of cake, jam side up, and the remaining filling. Top with the final cake and leave to set.

5 To make the ganache, heat the cream and chocolate in a pan over a low heat, stirring until the chocolate melts. Pour into a bowl, cool, then whisk until the mixture begins to hold its shape.

6 Spread the ganache smoothly over the sides and top of the cake. Decorate with chocolate curls scattered around the edge of the top, and arrange chocolate-dipped physalis in the centre. Store, chilled, until ready to serve.

CHOCOLATE-DIPPED PHYSALIS
Melt chocolate and dip each physalis into it. Leave to set on a baking sheet lined with baking parchment.

Nutritional information per portion: Energy 432kcal/1809kJ; Protein 4.7g; Carbohydrate 49.9g, of which sugars 38.4g; Fat 24.7g, of which saturates 14.9g; Cholesterol 57mg; Calcium 99mg; Fibre 1.4g; Sodium 120mg.

Devil's food cake

Originating in the US and dating back to 1905, this cake is always made using cocoa powder rather than melted chocolate. The chocolate cake is layered and covered with a fine white frosting flavoured with orange. It tastes very good indeed, and will keep for four days.

SERVES 10–12

175g/6oz/³⁄₄ cup butter, at room
    temperature, plus extra for greasing
50g/2oz/¹⁄₂ cup unsweetened cocoa powder
350g/12oz/scant 2 cups soft dark
    brown sugar
3 eggs
275g/10oz/1¹⁄₂ cups plain
    (all-purpose) flour
7.5ml/1¹⁄₂ tsp bicarbonate of soda
    (baking soda)

1.5ml/¹⁄₄ tsp baking powder
120ml/4fl oz/¹⁄₂ cup sour cream
shreds of orange rind, to decorate

FOR THE FROSTING
300g/11oz/1¹⁄₂ cups caster
    (superfine) sugar
2 egg whites
60ml/4 tbsp orange juice concentrate
15ml/1 tbsp lemon juice
grated rind of 1 orange

1 Preheat the oven to 180°C/350°F/Gas 4. Grease and line two 23cm/9in round shallow cake tins (pans) with baking parchment.

2 In a bowl, mix the cocoa powder with 175ml/6fl oz/³⁄₄ cup boiling water until smooth. Leave to cool.

3 Beat the butter and sugar until light and fluffy, then beat in the eggs one at a time. When the cocoa mixture is lukewarm, add it to the butter mixture. Sift the flour, bicarbonate of soda and baking powder into the cocoa mixture in three batches, alternating with the sour cream.

4 Pour into the tins and bake for 30–35 minutes. Leave to cool in the tins for 15 minutes, then turn out to cool on a wire rack to go cold. Remove the lining papers.

5 To make the frosting, put all the ingredients into a heatproof bowl set over a pan of gently simmering water. With an electric whisk, beat until the mixture holds soft peaks. Remove from the heat and continue beating until thick enough to spread. Quickly sandwich the cake layers with frosting, then spread over the top and sides. Decorate with orange rind shreds.

Nutritional information per portion: Energy 455kcal/1916kJ; Protein 5.7g; Carbohydrate 75.5g, of which sugars 57.6g; Fat 16.6g, of which saturates 9.6g; Cholesterol 84.6mg; Calcium 86.5mg; Fibre 1.2g; Sodium 165mg.

Chocolate and beetroot layer cake

Vegetables, like fruit, can add moisture to a cake, and although beetroot might seem like an unusual choice, it is actually wonderful for giving a cake depth of colour and a good consistency.

SERVES 10–12

115g/4oz/¹/₂ cup unsalted butter, softened,
   plus extra for greasing
unsweetened cocoa powder, for dusting
225g/8oz can cooked whole beetroot (beet),
   drained and juice reserved
425g/15oz/scant 2 cups soft light
   brown sugar
3 eggs
15ml/1 tbsp vanilla extract
75g/3oz dark (bittersweet) chocolate,
   melted and cooled
225g/8oz/2 cups plain (all-purpose) flour

10ml/2 tsp baking powder
pinch of salt
120ml/4fl oz/¹/₂ cup buttermilk
chocolate curls (optional), see page 82

FOR THE GANACHE

475ml/16fl oz/2 cups whipping cream or
   double (heavy) cream
500g/1¹/₄ lb dark (bittersweet) chocolate,
   broken into pieces
15ml/1 tbsp vanilla extract

1 Preheat the oven to 160°C/325°F/Gas 3. Grease two 23cm/9in round shallow cake tins (pans) and dust the base and sides with cocoa.

2 Grate the beetroot and add to the reserved juice. Set aside.

3 Using an electric whisk, beat the butter, sugar, eggs and vanilla extract in a bowl until pale. Reduce the speed and beat in the cooled melted chocolate. With the whisk on low speed, gradually beat the flour, baking powder and salt into the chocolate mixture, alternating with the buttermilk.

4 Add the beetroot and juice, then beat for 1 minute.

5 Divide between the prepared tins. Bake for 30–35 minutes, or until a skewer inserted in the centre of each cake comes out clean. Cool for 10 minutes in the tins, then turn out on to a wire rack to go cold. Remove the lining papers.

6 To make the ganache, heat the cream in a pan over medium heat, until it just begins to boil, stirring occasionally.

7 Remove from the heat and stir in the chocolate, stirring constantly until melted and smooth. Stir in the vanilla extract, then pour the mixture into a bowl.

8 Allow to cool, then chill, stirring every 10 minutes for about 1 hour, until the mixture thickens to a spreadable consistency.

9 To assemble the cake, put one layer on a serving plate and spread with one-third of the ganache. Put the second layer on top and spread the remaining ganache over the top and sides of the cake.

10 Decorate with the chocolate curls, if you like. Allow to set for 20–30 minutes, then chill until ready to serve. Any leftover cake can be frozen for up to 3 months.

Nutritional information per portion: Energy 699kcal/2925kJ; Protein 7.4g; Carbohydrate 85.1g, of which sugars 70.3g; Fat 38.9g, of which saturates 23.5g; Cholesterol 113mg; Calcium 109mg; Fibre 2.1g; Sodium 108mg.

Chocolate potato cake

This rich cake owes its moist texture to the addition of smooth mashed potato. Topped with chocolate fudge icing, the cake makes a superb dessert with a little whipped cream.

SERVES 10–12

225g/8oz/1 cup butter, plus extra
   for greasing
200g/7oz/1 cup caster (superfine) sugar
4 eggs, separated
175g/6oz dark (bittersweet) chocolate,
   finely grated
75g/3oz/³⁄₄ cup ground almonds
165g/5¹⁄₂oz/1¹⁄₂ cups mashed potato
225g/8oz/2 cup self-raising (self-rising) flour

5ml/1 tsp cinnamon
45ml/3 tbsp milk
chocolate curls, to decorate, see page 82
whipped cream, to serve

FOR THE ICING
115g/4oz dark (bittersweet) chocolate,
   broken into pieces
25g/1oz/2 tbsp butter, diced

1 Preheat the oven to 180°C/350°F/Gas 4. Grease and line a 23cm/9in round deep cake tin (pan) with baking parchment.

2 In a large bowl, cream together the butter and sugar until fluffy. Beat the egg yolks into the creamed mixture. Stir the chocolate into the creamed mixture with the ground almonds.

3 Pass the mashed potato through a sieve (strainer) or ricer, and stir it into the creamed chocolate mixture. Sift the flour and cinnamon and fold into the mixture with the milk.

4 Put the egg whites into a clean, grease-free bowl and whisk until stiff peaks form. Fold into the batter. Turn into the prepared tin. Bake for 1¼ hours, or until a skewer inserted into the cake comes out clean. Allow the cake to cool in the tin for 5 minutes. Turn out on to a wire rack to go cold. Peel off the paper.

5 To make the icing, melt the chocolate in a heatproof bowl over a pan of gently simmering water. Add the butter and stir until the mixture is smooth and glossy. Smooth the icing over the cake. Decorate with white and dark chocolate shavings. Allow to set. Serve with whipped cream.

Nutritional information per portion: Energy 575kcal/2403kJ; Protein 8.7g; Carbohydrate 59g, of which sugars 39g; Fat 35.5g, of which saturates 18.8g; Cholesterol 146mg; Calcium 141mg; Fibre 2.1g; Sodium 273mg.

Chocolate orange marquise

This fabulous cake has very little flour, but is rich with butter, eggs and chocolate, and flavoured with orange rind and juice. Enjoy this special cake with coffee, or with cream as a dessert. Store chilled in an airtight container for up to three days.

SERVES 6–8

225g/8oz/1 cup unsalted butter, diced, at
  room temperature, plus extra for greasing
200g/7oz/1 cup caster (superfine) sugar
60ml/4 tbsp freshly squeezed orange juice
350g/12oz plain (semisweet) chocolate,
  broken into pieces

5 eggs
finely grated rind of 1 orange
45ml/3 tbsp plain (all-purpose) flour
icing (confectioners') sugar, to decorate
finely pared strips of orange rind, to decorate

1 Preheat the oven to 180°C/350°F/Gas 4. Grease and line a 23cm/9in round deep cake tin (pan) with baking parchment.

2 Put 115g/4oz/generous ½ cup of the caster sugar in a heavy pan with the fresh orange juice. Place over a low heat until all the sugar has dissolved. Stir constantly so that the sugar does not catch and burn. Do not allow to boil.

3 Remove from the heat and stir in the chocolate until melted, then add the butter, stirring, until melted and evenly mixed. Cool.

4 Put the eggs with the remaining sugar in a large bowl and whisk until pale and very thick. Add the orange rind. Using a metal spoon, fold the chocolate mixture lightly and evenly into the egg mixture using a metal spoon and a figure-of-eight motion. Sift the flour over and fold in evenly.

5 Scrape the mixture into the prepared tin. Put the tin into a roasting pan, then pour hot water into the roasting pan to reach half-way up the outside of the cake tin.

6 Bake for 1 hour, or until the cake is firm to the touch. Carefully remove the cake tin from the roasting pan and cool for 15–20 minutes. Invert the cake on a baking sheet. Lift away the tin and lining paper. Place a serving plate over the cake, then turn the baking sheet and plate over as one so that the cake is transferred to the plate.

7 Dust with icing sugar, decorate with strips of pared orange rind and serve slightly warm or cold.

Nutritional information per portion: Energy 553'Kcal/2309kJ; Protein 3.1g; Carbohydrate 59.1g, of which sugars 54.4g; Fat 35.5g, of which saturates 22g; Cholesterol 63mg; Calcium 41mg; Fibre 1.3g; Sodium 176mg.

Sachertorte

This glorious gateau dates back to 1832, when it was created by Franz Sacher, a chef of the royal household in Vienna. It is rich and dark, with an apricot glaze and a rich, glossy topping.

SERVES 10–12

150g/5oz/10 tbsp unsalted butter, plus extra
    for greasing
115g/4oz/generous ¹/₂ cup caster
    (superfine) sugar
8 eggs, separated
225g/8oz dark (bittersweet) chocolate,
    melted and cooled
115g/4oz/1 cup plain (all-purpose) flour

FOR THE GLAZE
225g/8oz/1 cup apricot jam
15ml/1 tbsp lemon juice

FOR THE ICING
225g/8oz dark (bittersweet) chocolate,
    broken into pieces
200g/7oz/1 cup caster (superfine) sugar
15ml/1 tbsp golden (light corn) syrup
250ml/8fl oz/1 cup double (heavy) cream
5ml/1 tsp vanilla extract
chocolate curls, to decorate, see page 82

1 Preheat the oven to 180°C/350°F/Gas 4. Grease and line a 23cm/9in round deep cake tin (pan). Beat the butter with the sugar until fluffy, then add the egg yolks, one at a time, beating after each addition. Beat in the melted chocolate, then sift the flour over the mixture and fold it in evenly.

2 Put the egg whites into a clean, grease-free bowl and whisk until they form stiff peaks. Stir about a quarter of the whites into the chocolate mixture to lighten it, then fold in the remaining whites. Pour the mixture into the prepared tin and smooth the top level. Bake for 50–55 minutes, or until firm.

3 Leave in the tin for 5 minutes, then turn out on to a wire rack to go cold. Remove the lining paper. Slice in half across the middle. To make the glaze, heat the jam with the lemon juice in a pan until melted, then strain into a bowl. Brush the top and sides of each layer with the glaze, then sandwich them together. Put the cake on a wire rack.

4 To make the icing, put the chocolate, sugar, golden syrup, cream and vanilla extract in a pan. Heat gently, stirring constantly, until the mixture is thick and smooth. Simmer for 4 minutes, without stirring, until the mixture registers 95°C/200°F on a sugar thermometer. Pour over the cake to cover the top and sides. Leave to set, decorate with chocolate curls.

Nutritional information per portion: Energy 625kcal/2618kJ; Protein 7.6g; Carbohydrate 73.1g, of which sugars 65.5g; Fat 35.8g, of which saturates 20.8g; Cholesterol 184mg; Calcium 73mg; Fibre 1.2g; Sodium 143mg.

Dessert Cakes and Cheesecakes

If you want a spectacular cake to serve as a grand finale to a meal, a dessert cake or cheesecake is the perfect choice. These cakes look impressive but are actually simple to make, and cakes such as Cinnamon Apple Gateau or Sponge Cake with Strawberries and Cream have a wonderful combination of fruit, sponge and cream. Baked Coffee Cheesecake and Rum and Raisin Cheesecake are both delicious and are ideal to make ahead of time.

Chocolate brandy-snap gateau

Savour every mouthful of this sensational dark chocolate gateau. The cake is rich with chocolate and hazelnuts, then filled and topped with ganache – a cream and chocolate icing. Crisp brandy-snap frills look wonderful and contrast beautifully with the soft cake. Eat fresh.

SERVES 8

225g/8oz/1 cup unsalted butter, softened,
  plus extra for greasing
225g/8oz plain (semisweet) chocolate,
  broken into pieces
200g/7oz/scant 1 cup muscovado
  (molasses) sugar
6 eggs, separated
5ml/1 tsp vanilla extract
150g/5oz/1¼ cups ground hazelnuts
60ml/4 tbsp fresh white breadcrumbs
finely grated rind of 1 large orange
icing (confectioners') sugar, for dusting

FOR THE BRANDY SNAPS
50g/2oz/¼ cup unsalted butter
50g/2oz/¼ cup caster (superfine) sugar
75g/3oz/¼ cup golden (light corn) syrup
50g/2oz/½ cup plain (all-purpose) flour
5ml/1 tsp brandy

FOR THE CHOCOLATE GANACHE
250ml/8fl oz/1 cup double (heavy) cream
225g/8oz plain (semisweet) chocolate,
  broken into pieces

1 Preheat the oven to 180°C/250°F/Gas 4. Grease and line two 20cm/8in round shallow cake tins (pans) and two baking sheets with baking parchment.

2 To make the cake, melt the chocolate in a heatproof bowl set over a pan of gently simmering water. Stir occasionally. Remove from the heat to cool.

3 Beat the butter and sugar in a large bowl until pale and fluffy. Beat in the egg yolks and vanilla extract. Add the melted chocolate and mix thoroughly.

4 Put the egg whites into a clean, grease-free bowl and whisk until they form soft peaks. Fold a tablespoon of the whites into the chocolate mixture to slacken it, then fold in the rest in batches with the ground hazelnuts, breadcrumbs and orange rind. Divide the cake batter between the prepared tins and smooth the tops level. Bake for 25–30 minutes, or until well risen and firm, then turn out to cool on wire racks. Remove the lining paper.

5 To make the brandy snaps, melt the butter, sugar and syrup in a pan over a low heat, stirring occasionally. Remove from the heat and stir in the flour and brandy until smooth.

6 Place small spoonfuls well apart on the baking sheet leaving enough space to allow each biscuit to spread out, and bake for 10–15 minutes, or until golden.

7 Cool for a few seconds until firm enough to lift. Immediately pinch the edges of each brandy snap to make a frilled effect. If the biscuits become too firm, pop them back into the oven for a few minutes. Leave to set on a wire rack.

8 Meanwhile, to make the chocolate ganache, heat the cream and chocolate together in a pan over a low heat, stirring frequently until the chocolate has melted. Pour into a bowl. Leave to cool, then stir until the mixture begins to hold its shape.

9 Sandwich the cake layers together with half the chocolate ganache, transfer to a plate and spread the remaining ganache on top. Arrange the brandy snap frills over the gateau and dust with icing sugar. Serve immediately.

Nutritional information per portion: Energy 870kcal/3622kJ; Protein 10.7g; Carbohydrate 70g, of which sugars 59g; Fat 62.7g, of which saturates 31.2g; Cholesterol 244mg; Calcium 102mg; Fibre 2.3g; Sodium 424mg.

Layer cake

Three light cakes enclose a layer of crushed raspberries and one of custard, then the whole cake is covered with vanilla-flavoured cream. Make when raspberries are at their sweetest and best.

SERVES 10–12

115g/4oz/½ cup unsalted butter, plus extra
    for greasing
200g/7oz/1 cup caster (superfine) sugar
4 eggs, separated
45ml/3 tbsp milk
175g/6oz/1½ cups plain (all-purpose) flour
25ml/1½ tbsp cornflour (cornstarch)
7.5ml/1½ tsp baking powder
5ml/1 tsp vanilla sugar
fresh raspberries, to decorate

FOR THE CUSTARD FILLING
2 eggs
90g/3½oz/½ cup caster (superfine) sugar

15ml/1 tbsp cornflour (cornstarch)
350ml/12fl oz/1½ cups milk

FOR THE CREAM TOPPING
475ml/16fl oz/2 cups double (heavy) cream
    or whipping cream
25g/1oz/½ cup icing (confectioners') sugar
5ml/1 tsp vanilla sugar

FOR THE RASPBERRY FILLING
375g/13oz/generous 2 cups raspberries
sugar, to taste

1 Preheat the oven to 230°C/450°F/Gas 8. Lightly grease and flour three 23cm/9in shallow cake tins (pans).

2 Cream the butter with the sugar in a large bowl until light and fluffy. Beat in the egg yolks, one at a time. Stir in the milk until blended.

3 In a separate bowl, sift together the flour, cornflour, baking powder and vanilla sugar. Beat the flour mixture into the egg mixture.

4 Put the egg whites into a clean, grease-free bowl and whisk until they form stiff peaks. Gently fold the egg whites into the cake mixture.

5 Divide the batter evenly among the tins and smooth to the edges. Bake for 12 minutes. Leave the cakes to cool for 10 minutes, then turn out to go cold on a wire rack.

6 To make the custard filling, whisk together the eggs and sugar in a pan. Whisk in the cornflour and the milk. Cook over a low heat, stirring, until thickened. Remove from the heat and leave to cool.

7 To make the cream topping, beat the cream in a bowl until soft peaks form. Stir in the icing sugar and vanilla sugar and continue beating until stiff.

8 To make the raspberry filling, crush the raspberries in a bowl and add a little sugar to taste. To assemble the cake, place one layer on a serving plate and spread with the raspberry filling.

9 Place a second cake layer over the first and spread with the cooled custard. Top with the final layer. Spread whipped cream over the sides and top of the cake. Chill the cake until ready to serve, and decorate with raspberries.

Nutritional information per portion: Energy 433kcal/1811kJ; Protein 6.1g; Carbohydrate 44.6g, of which sugars 30.4g; Fat 27g, of which saturates 15.9g; Cholesterol 157mg; Calcium 86mg; Fibre 1.2g; Sodium 109mg.

Polish cheesecake

There are many different versions of cheesecake. Unlike others, this rich, creamy baked version is not made on a biscuit base, but includes raisins and semolina, giving it sweetness and a firm texture. Keep this cheesecake refrigerated for two days, and freeze for up to two months.

SERVES 6–8

100g/3¾oz/scant ½ cup butter,
   softened, plus extra for greasing
500g/1¼lb/2¼ cups curd cheese
2.5ml/½ tsp vanilla extract
6 eggs, separated
150g/5½oz/scant ¾ cup caster
   (superfine) sugar
10ml/2 tsp grated lemon rind
15ml/1 tbsp cornflour (cornstarch)
15ml/1 tbsp semolina
50g/2oz/⅓ cup raisins
icing (confectioners') sugar, for dusting

1 Preheat the oven to 200°C/400°F/ Gas 6. Grease and line the base and sides of a 20cm/8in loose-based cake tin (pan) with baking parchment.

2 In a large bowl, cream together the curd cheese, butter and vanilla extract.

3 Put the egg whites into a clean, grease-free bowl and add 15ml/1 tbsp sugar. Whisk until the whites form stiff peaks.

4 Whisk the egg yolks with the remaining sugar until thick and creamy. Add to the cheese mixture with the lemon rind, and stir to combine.

5 Gently fold in the egg whites, then fold in the cornflour, semolina and raisins.

6 Transfer to the lined tin and bake for 1 hour, or until the cake is set and golden brown.

7 Leave to cool in the tin. Remove the sides of the tin and papers, then dust with icing sugar and serve.

Nutritional information per portion: Energy 347kcal/ 1488kJ; Protein 10.8g; Carbohydrate 24.8g, of which sugars 21.6g; Fat23.6g, of which saturates 13.4g; Cholesterol 196mg; Calcium 34mg; Fibre 0g; Sodium131mg.

Baked coffee cheesecake

This rich, baked and chilled cheesecake, flavoured with coffee and orange liqueur, has a wonderfully dense, velvety texture and makes a lovely dessert served with single cream. Keep for two days refrigerated. Freeze for up to two months.

SERVES 8

75g/3oz/6 tbsp butter, plus extra for greasing
115g/4oz/1 cup plain (all-purpose) flour
5ml/1 tsp baking powder
50g/2oz/¼ cup caster (superfine) sugar
1 egg, lightly beaten
30ml/2 tbsp cold water
single (light) cream, to serve

FOR THE FILLING

45ml/3 tbsp near-boiling water
30ml/2 tbsp ground coffee
4 eggs
225g/8oz/generous 1 cup caster (superfine) sugar
450g/1lb/2 cups cream cheese, at room temperature
30ml/2 tbsp orange liqueur
40g/1½ oz/⅓ cup plain (all-purpose) flour, sifted
300ml/½ pint/1¼ cups whipping cream
30ml/2 tbsp icing (confectioners') sugar, for dusting

1 Preheat the oven to 160°C/325°F/Gas 3. Grease and line a 20cm/8in round loose-based cake tin (pan) with baking parchment.

2 Sift the flour and baking powder into a bowl. Rub in the butter until the mixture resembles fine crumbs.

3 Stir in the sugar, then add the egg and the cold water, and mix to a dough. Press the mixture into the base of the tin.

4 For the filling, pour the water over the coffee and leave for 4 minutes. Strain through a fine sieve (strainer).

5 Whisk the eggs and sugar until thick.

6 Using a wooden spoon, beat the cream cheese until softened. Beat in the liqueur, a spoonful at a time.

7 Gradually mix in the whisked eggs. Fold in the flour. Stir in the whipping cream and coffee. Pour over the base and bake for 1½ hours. Turn off the heat. Leave in the oven to go cold with the oven door ajar.

8 Chill for 1 hour. Remove from the tin and dust with icing sugar.

Nutritional information per portion: Energy 713kcal/2969kJ; Protein 8.4g; Carbohydrate 53.4g, of which sugars 38.6g; Fat 52.8g, of which saturates 32g; Cholesterol 233mg; Calcium 143mg; Fibre 0.6g; Sodium 301mg.

Rum and raisin cheesecake

Spectacular to look at, and superb to eat, this light, rum-flavoured cheesecake is studded with raisins and surrounded by diagonal stripes of plain and chocolate sponge.

SERVES 8–10

115g/4oz/¹⁄₂ cup unsalted butter, melted,
    plus extra for greasing
2 eggs
50g/2oz/¹⁄₄ cup caster (superfine) sugar
50g/2oz/¹⁄₂ cup plain (all-purpose)
    flour, sifted
5ml/1 tsp unsweetened cocoa powder,
    mixed to a paste with 15ml/1 tbsp hot
    water and cooled
225g/8oz ginger biscuits
    (gingersnaps), crushed
**whipped cream and sifted unsweetened
    cocoa powder, to decorate**

FOR THE FILLING
45ml/3 tbsp water
1 sachet powdered gelatine
300ml/¹⁄₂ pint/1¹⁄₄ cups double
    (heavy) cream
30ml/2 tbsp milk
75g/3oz/generous ¹⁄₂ cup raisins
60ml/4 tbsp rum
50g/2oz/¹⁄₂ cup icing (confectioners')
    sugar, sifted
450g/1lb/2 cups curd cheese

1 Preheat the oven to 200°C/400°F/Gas 6. Grease and line a 28 × 18cm/ 11 × 7in Swiss roll tin (jelly roll pan) with baking parchment. Also, grease and line a 20cm/8in round loose-based cake tin (pan). Cover a wire rack with baking parchment.

2 Mix the eggs and sugar in a heatproof bowl. Put over a pan of barely simmering water and whisk until the mixture forms a thick trail. Fold in the sifted flour using a metal spoon.

3 Spoon half the mixture into a large piping bag fitted with a 4cm/1¹⁄₂in star nozzle, or use a paper piping (pastry) bag and cut the end off. Pipe diagonal stripes of the cake mixture across the Swiss roll tin, leaving an equal space between each row. Stir the cooled cocoa paste into the remaining cake mixture until evenly mixed. Fill a piping bag with the batter and pipe as before, filling the gaps to give rows of alternating colours.

4 Bake for 10–12 minutes, then turn out the sponge on to the paper-topped wire rack. Peel off the lining paper. Leave to go cold.

5 Mix the melted butter and crushed ginger biscuits in a bowl. Spread over the bottom of the round cake tin and press down firmly. Cut the sponge in half lengthways and arrange the two strips around the sides of the cake tin. Set aside.

6 To make the filling, put the water into a small heatproof bowl and sprinkle over the gelatine. Leave until spongy. Put the bowl over a pan of barely simmering water and stir until the gelatine dissolves. Remove from the heat and leave to cool slightly. Whisk the cream with the milk in a bowl. Fold in the raisins, rum, icing sugar and curd cheese, then stir in the cooled gelatine. Spoon the filling into the prepared tin and chill until set.

7 To serve, carefully remove the cheesecake from the tin and place on a serving plate. Trim the cake level with the filling. Dust with cocoa powder and pipe whirls of cream around the edge.

Nutritional information per portion: Energy 467kcal/1946kJ; Protein 10.5g; Carbohydrate 34.6g, of which sugars 21.1g; Fat 33.3g, of which saturates 19.5g; Cholesterol 114mg; Calcium 121mg; Fibre 0.6g; Sodium 389mg.

Cinnamon apple gateau

Make this cake for an autumn celebration. A light sponge is split and filled with a honey and cream cheese layer as well as softly cooked cinnamon apples and sultanas, then topped with glazed apples. Keep the sponge, unfilled, for two days in an airtight container; fill and eat it fresh.

SERVES 8–10

butter, for greasing
3 eggs
115g/4oz/generous 1/2 cup caster
   (superfine) sugar
75g/3oz/2/3 cup plain (all-purpose) flour
5ml/1 tsp ground cinnamon

FOR THE FILLING AND TOPPING
4 large eating apples
60ml/4 tbsp clear honey

75g/3oz/generous 1/2 cup sultanas
   (golden raisins)
2.5ml/1/2 tsp ground cinnamon
350g/12oz/11/2 cups soft cheese
60ml/4 tbsp fromage frais or crème fraîche
10ml/2 tsp lemon juice
45ml/3 tbsp apricot jam, strained
mint sprigs, to decorate

1 Preheat the oven to 190°C/375°F/Gas 5. Grease and line a 23cm/9in round cake tin (pan) with baking parchment.

2 Put the eggs and sugar in a bowl and beat with an electric whisk until thick and mousse-like and the beaters leave a trail on the surface.

3 Sift the flour and cinnamon over the egg mixture and carefully fold in with a large spoon.

4 Pour into the prepared tin and bake for 25–30 minutes, or until the cake springs back when lightly pressed in the centre.

5 Slide a knife between the cake and the tin to loosen the edge, then turn the cake on to a wire rack to cool.

6 To make the filling, peel, core and slice three apples and put them in a pan. Add 30ml/ 2 tbsp of the honey and 15ml/1 tbsp water. Cover and cook over a low heat for 10 minutes, or until the apples have softened.

7 Add the sultanas and cinnamon, stir, replace the lid and leave to cool.

8 Put the soft cheese in a bowl with the remaining honey, the fromage frais or crème fraîche and half the lemon juice. Beat until smooth.

9 Cut the cake into two equal rounds. Put half on a plate and drizzle over any liquid from the apple mixture.

10 Spread with two-thirds of the cheese mixture, then top with the apple filling. Fit the top of the cake in place.

11 Swirl the remaining cheese mixture over the top of the sponge. Core and slice the remaining apple, sprinkle with lemon juice and use to decorate the edge of the cake. Brush the apple with apricot glaze and place mint sprigs on top to decorate.

Nutritional information per portion: Energy 239kcal/1010kJ; Protein 10.8g; Carbohydrate 39.9g, of which sugars 32.8g; Fat 5.8g, of which saturates 2.9g; Cholesterol 82mg; Calcium 97mg; Fibre 1.1g; Sodium 225mg.

Sponge cake with strawberries and cream

This classic summer treat is filled with ripe, fragrant strawberries. To ensure a perfect sponge, have all the ingredients at room temperature. Eat this cake on the day it is made.

SERVES 8–10

oil, for greasing

115g/4oz/generous ½ cup caster
  (superfine) sugar, plus extra for dusting

90g/3½oz/¾ cup plain (all-purpose) flour,
  sifted, plus extra for dusting

4 eggs

icing (confectioners') sugar, for dusting

FOR THE FILLING

300ml/½ pint/1¼ cups double
  (heavy) cream

about 5ml/1 tsp icing (confectioners')
  sugar, sifted

450g/1lb/4 cups strawberries, washed
  and hulled

a little orange liqueur (optional)

1 Preheat the oven to 190°C/375°F/Gas 5. Grease a round 20cm/8in cake tin (pan). Dust the tin with 10ml/2 tsp caster sugar and flour combined. Tap out the excess.

2 Put the eggs and sugar into a bowl and use an electric whisk at high speed until the mixture is light and thick, and the mixture leaves a trail as it drops from the whisk.

3 Sift the flour over the eggs and fold it in with a metal spoon, mixing well without losing volume. Pour into the cake tin. Bake for 25–30 minutes, or until the sponge feels springy. Leave in the tin for 5 minutes, loosen with a knife and invert on to a wire rack to go cold.

4 To make the filling, whip the cream with a little icing sugar until it is stiff enough to hold its shape. Slice the sponge across the middle to make two even layers. Divide half the cream between the two inner cut sides. Reserve some strawberries for the cake top, and then slice the rest. Put one sponge half on a plate and arrange the strawberries on the cream. Sprinkle with liqueur, if using.

5 Cover with the second cake half and press down gently. Spread the remaining cream on top of the cake, and arrange the reserved strawberries, whole or halved according to size, on top.

6 Set aside for an hour or so for the flavours to develop, then dust lightly with icing sugar. Serve.

Nutritional information per portion: Energy 333kcal/1387kJ; Protein 5.3g; Carbohydrate 27.8g, of which sugars 19.2g; Fat 23.1g, of which saturates 13.3g; Cholesterol 147mg; Calcium 65mg; Fibre 1g; Sodium 48mg.

Princess cake

A light sponge cake is layered and topped with vanilla custard cream, then covered with home-made marzipan to make an unusual and special dessert gateau. You can make the marzipan in advance, if you like. Serve a slice of the cake with strawberries. Keep for two days in a cool place.

SERVES 8–10

200g/7oz/scant 1 cup unsalted butter, plus
   extra for greasing
400g/14oz/2 cups caster (superfine) sugar
3 eggs
350g/12oz/3 cups plain (all-purpose) flour
5ml/1 tsp baking powder
10ml/2 tsp vanilla sugar
fresh strawberries, to serve

FOR THE FILLING AND TOPPING

3 gelatine leaves
1 litre/1¾ pints/4 cups double
   (heavy) cream
10ml/2 tsp sugar
10ml/2 tsp cornflour (cornstarch)
2 egg yolks
10ml/2 tsp vanilla sugar

FOR THE MARZIPAN

200g/7oz/1¾ cups ground almonds
200g/7oz/1¾ cups icing
   (confectioners') sugar
1 egg white
a few drops of green food colour

1 To make the marzipan, put the ground almonds in a bowl and add the icing sugar and egg white. Mix to form a paste.

2 Add a few drops of green food colour and knead until evenly coloured. Refrigerate in a plastic bag for up to 3 days until required.

3 Preheat the oven to 180°C/350°F/Gas 4. Grease and line a 20cm/8in round cake tin (pan).

4 Put the butter and sugar in a large bowl and beat until fluffy. Add the eggs and whisk together. Sift in the flour, baking powder and vanilla sugar and stir together.

5 Spoon the batter into the cake tin and bake for 1 hour, or until firm to the touch. Leave to cool in the tin. When cold, slice in half horizontally.

6 To make the filling, soak the gelatine in cold water according to the directions on the packet. Put half of the cream, the sugar, cornflour and egg yolks in a pan and heat gently, stirring constantly, until the mixture thickens. Do not allow it to boil or the eggs will curdle.

7 Pour into a bowl, and stir in the soaked gelatine leaves. Leave to cool.

8 Put the remaining cream with the vanilla sugar in a bowl and whisk until stiff. Fold into the cooled custard and quickly spread half the mixture over the bottom layer of cake. Put the other cake layer on top and spread the remaining custard over the top and sides.

9 Put the marzipan between two sheets of foil. Roll out a thin round. Remove the top sheet of foil and, using a 30cm/12in diameter plate as a guide, cut a marzipan circle. Use the foil to lift the marzipan circle over the top of the cake and smooth it down the sides. Trim the edge around the cake base. Decorate with fresh strawberries.

Nutritional information per portion: Energy 1326kcal/5512kJ; Protein 11.3g; Carbohydrate 112g, of which sugars 77.6g; Fat 95.7g, of which saturates 56.1g; Cholesterol 346mg; Calcium 191mg; Fibre 1.9g; Sodium 218mg.

Coconut lime gateau

American frosting is what makes this zesty lime and coconut gateau so attractive. Made by whisking egg white and a sugar mixture over heat, the frosting is like a soft meringue icing. It tastes divine scattered with toasted coconut. Eat the gateau fresh or refrigerate it for two days.

SERVES 10–12

225g/8oz/1 cup butter, at room
    temperature, plus extra for greasing
225g/8oz/2 cups plain (all-purpose) flour
12.5ml/2¹⁄₂ tsp baking powder
225g/8oz/generous 1 cup caster
    (superfine) sugar
grated rind of 2 limes
4 eggs
60ml/4 tbsp fresh lime juice (from about
    2 limes)
85g/3oz/1 cup desiccated (dry unsweetened
    shredded) coconut

FOR THE FROSTING

275g/10oz/scant 1¹⁄₂ cups caster
    (superfine) sugar
2.5ml/¹⁄₂ tsp cream of tartar
2 egg whites
60ml/4 tbsp cold water
15ml/1 tbsp liquid glucose
10ml/2 tsp vanilla extract

1 Preheat the oven to 180°C/350°F/Gas 4. Grease and line two 23cm/9in round shallow cake tins (pans) with baking parchment.

2 Sift together the flour and baking powder into a bowl.

3 In another large bowl, beat the butter until soft. Add the sugar and lime rind, then beat until pale and fluffy. Beat in the eggs, one at a time, adding 5ml/1 tsp of the flour mixture with each addition to stop the batter from curdling. Beat the mixture well between each addition.

4 Using a wooden spoon, fold in the flour mixture in small batches, alternating with the lime juice. When the batter is smooth, stir in two-thirds of the coconut.

5 Divide the batter between the tins and spread it evenly to the sides.

6 Bake for 30–35 minutes, or until a skewer inserted into the centre comes out clean. Leave to cool in the tins for 10 minutes, then turn out to cool on a wire rack. Remove the lining paper. Leave to go cold.

7 Spread the remaining coconut in another cake tin. Bake until golden brown, stirring occasionally. Watch carefully so that the coconut does not get too dark. Allow to cool in the tin.

8 To make the frosting, put the sugar in a large heatproof bowl and add the cream of tartar, egg whites, water and glucose. Stir to mix. Set the bowl over a pan of boiling water. Beat with an electric whisk at high speed for 7 minutes or until thick and stiff peaks form. Remove from the heat.

9 Add the vanilla extract and continue beating for 3 minutes or until the frosting has cooled slightly.

10 Invert one cake on a serving plate. Spread a layer of frosting on top. Set the second cake on top. Swirl the rest of the frosting all over the cake. Sprinkle with the toasted coconut and leave to set.

Nutritional information per portion: Energy 732kcal/3079kJ; Protein 7.3g; Carbohydrate 111g, of which sugars 59g; Fat 32g, of which saturates 20.5g; Cholesterol 155mg; Calcium 105.7mg; Fibre 2.1g; Sodium 221mg.

Lemon chiffon cake

Split a light lemon sponge cake in half horizontally, then fill with a lovely thick layer of lemon mousse to give it a tangy centre. Top with a lemon icing and lemon zest and you have the most lemony cake. Keep this for one day in the refrigerator, or freeze for two months, undecorated.

SERVES 8

butter, for greasing
2 eggs
75g/3oz/6 tbsp caster (superfine) sugar
grated rind of 1 lemon
50g/2oz/½ cup plain (all-purpose)
    flour, sifted
lemon shreds, to decorate

FOR THE FILLING
2 eggs, separated
75g/3oz/6 tbsp caster (superfine) sugar

grated rind and juice of 1 lemon
15ml/1 tbsp gelatine
120ml/4fl oz/½ cup fromage frais or
    crème fraîche

FOR THE ICING
15ml/1 tbsp lemon juice
115g/4oz/1 cup icing (confectioners')
    sugar, sifted

1 Preheat the oven to 180°C/350°F/Gas 4. Grease and line a 20cm/8in round loose-based cake tin (pan).

2 Whisk the eggs, sugar and lemon rind until mousse-like. Fold in the flour, then pour into the cake tin.

3 Bake for 20–25 minutes, or until the cake springs back when lightly pressed in the centre. Turn on to a rack to go cold. Clean the cake tin.

4 Remove the lining paper. Split the cake in half horizontally and return the lower half to the clean cake tin.

5 To make the filling, put the egg yolks, sugar, lemon rind and juice in a bowl. Beat with an electric whisk until thick, pale and creamy.

6 Pour 30ml/2 tbsp water into a small heatproof bowl and sprinkle the gelatine on top. Leave until spongy, then set the bowl over simmering water and stir until dissolved. Cool slightly, then whisk into the yolk mixture. Fold in the fromage frais or crème fraîche.

7 When the filling mixture begins to set, whisk the egg whites in a clean, grease-free bowl until they form soft peaks. Stir a spoonful into the mousse mixture to lighten it, then fold in the rest.

8 Pour the filling over the sponge in the cake tin, spreading it to the edges. Put the second layer of sponge on top and chill until set.

9 Slide a knife dipped in hot water between the tin and the cake to loosen it, then transfer the cake to a serving plate.

10 To make the icing, add enough lemon juice to the icing sugar to make a thick, spreadable icing. Pour over the cake and spread to the edges. Decorate with lemon shreds.

Nutritional information per portion: Energy 356kcal/1491kJ; Protein 6.7g; Carbohydrate 43.6g, of which sugars 29.8g; Fat 18.4g, of which saturates 4g; Cholesterol 118mg; Calcium 68mg; Fibre 0.6g; Sodium 227mg.

Special Occasion Cakes

A centrepiece cake is a must at any celebration such as a christening, a wedding or the festive days of Easter or Christmas. Most of the cakes here can be made ahead, and decorative techniques are clearly explained. Start off with simple projects: Easy Birthday Cake and Chocolate Drizzle Party Cake, which is simple to decorate but looks so impressive. Try a Traditional Christmas Cake or the light zesty version – White Christmas Cake.

Lemon daisy christening cake

This delicate sponge cake is drizzled with a lemon syrup, making it moist with good keeping qualities. Use sugarpaste to give it the perfect finish, and decorate with hand-moulded daisies.

SERVES 16–18

350g/12oz/1½ cups butter or block
    margarine, plus extra for greasing
350g/12oz/1¾ cups caster (superfine) sugar
6 eggs, beaten
115g/4oz/1 cup plain (all-purpose) flour
275g/10oz/2½ cups self-raising
    (self-rising) flour
finely grated rind and juice of 2 lemons

FOR THE SYRUP AND DECORATIONS

100g/3¼ oz/generous ½ cup caster
    (superfine) sugar
finely grated rind and juice of 2 lemons
1 quantity buttercream icing, see page 218
icing (confectioners') sugar, for dusting
1kg/2¼lb sugarpaste icing, see page 221
yellow and pink edible paste food colourings
small tube writing icing
Materials: wide satin ribbon

1 Preheat the oven to 160°C/325°F/Gas 3. Grease and line a 23cm/9in deep, round cake tin (pan) with baking parchment.

2 In a bowl, beat the butter and sugar together until light and fluffy. Gradually beat in the eggs a little at a time, adding 5ml/1 tsp flour with each addition to prevent the mixture from curdling. Sift the flours into the bowl and fold into the egg mixture with the lemon rind and juice until smooth.

3 Spoon into the tin and smooth the top level. Bake for 1¼ hours, or until a warmed skewer inserted into the middle comes out clean. Leave in the tin until just warm, then prick over the top of the cake with a skewer.

4 To make the syrup, put the sugar, lemon juice and rind in a pan and heat gently until the sugar dissolves completely. Allow to cool slightly. Brush the syrup over the cake and leave to cool completely in the tin. Remove the lining paper. Wrap the cake in baking parchment, then in foil.

5 Cut the cake in half horizontally, sandwich together with buttercream icing, then spread the remainder thinly around the outside.

6 Put the sugarpaste icing on a surface lightly dusted with icing sugar, and roll out to a circle large enough to cover the top and sides of the cake. Lift the sugarpaste over the cake, smooth down with your hands to remove any bubbles or pleats, then trim the excess away carefully with a sharp knife.

7 Roll the trimmings into small pea-sized balls, then shape each into a cone. Flatten one edge thinly. Using clean scissors, snip the edge to form petals. Mark the centre with the scissor points.

8 Put a dot each of yellow and pink paste colours on to a plate and, using a paintbrush, dilute slightly with water. Paint the centres of the flowers lemon and the outer petal tips pale pink. Leave to dry out. Position the flowers on the cake in a daisy circle and stick each in place using a little blob of writing icing.

9 Write the name or message in the centre of the cake, if you like, and finish by tying a deep ribbon in a bow around the sides of the cake.

Nutritional information per portion: Energy 591kcal/2503kJ; Protein 5.5g; Carbohydrate 117.6g, of which sugars 108.3g; Fat 11.6g, of which saturates 2.4g; Cholesterol 38mg; Calcium 112mg; Fibre 2g; Sodium 140mg.

Chocolate drizzle party cake

Make this moist chocolate and hazelnut cake to celebrate almost any family occasion. The decoration couldn't be simpler, but it looks effective. The cake is easy to make, children and adults love it, and it can even be served with fresh summer fruits or a scoop of ice cream.

SERVES 10

115g/4oz/¹/₂ cup butter, softened, plus
   extra for greasing

175g/6oz/scant 1 cup natural caster
   (superfine) sugar

4 large (US extra large) eggs, separated

175g/6oz/1¹/₂ cups self-raising (self-rising)
   flour, sifted

115g/4oz plain (semisweet)
   chocolate, grated

90ml/6 tbsp milk

115g/4oz/1 cup ground hazelnuts

FOR THE FILLING AND TOPPING

60ml/4 tbsp chocolate and hazelnut
   spread, warmed

200g/7oz milk chocolate

150g/5oz white chocolate

edible gold or silver balls

Materials: wired silver ribbon

1 Preheat the oven to 220°C/425°F/Gas 7. Grease and line a 20cm/8in deep round cake tin (pan) with baking parchment.

2 Beat the butter and sugar until light and fluffy, then whisk in the egg yolks gradually, adding 5ml/1 tsp flour with each addition. Stir in the grated chocolate, milk and hazelnuts.

3 Whisk the egg whites until they form soft peaks. Fold them into the mixture, alternating with the remaining flour. Spoon into the tin and smooth level. Reduce the oven temperature to 170°C/350°F/Gas 3. Bake in the centre of the oven for about 1 hour 10 minutes.

4 Cool in the tin for 5 minutes, then turn out to cool on a wire rack and peel away the lining paper. Cut the cake in half, and cover one half with warmed chocolate spread. Sandwich the other half on top and put them on to a serving plate.

5 Melt the chocolates in two separate heatproof bowls set over pans of simmering water, then spoon into separate small paper piping (pastry) bags. Snip off the end of each bag and drizzle each chocolate over the top and side of the cake. Sprinkle the edible gold or silver balls over the top and leave to set for 1 hour. Finish with a large wired bow in the centre of the cake.

Nutritional information per portion: Energy 430kcal/1790kJ; Protein 7.8g; Carbohydrate 29.5g, of which sugars 28.8g; Fat 32.1g, of which saturates 13.6g; Cholesterol 96mg; Calcium 92mg; Fibre 1.9g; Sodium 125mg.

Celebration bow cake

Adding a little glycerine to this delicate almond cake helps it retain its moisture for longer, so you can make it ahead of time. The cake is ideal for any type of celebration, and you can vary the icing colours to suit. Small icing cutters are useful for quick-and-easy cake decorating.

SERVES 12

275g/10oz/2½ cups self-raising
   (self-rising) flour
2.5ml/½ tsp baking powder
50g/2oz/¼ cup ground almonds
275g/10oz/1¼ cups soft tub margarine,
   plus extra for greasing
275g/10oz/scant 1½ cups natural caster
   (superfine) sugar
5 eggs, beaten
a few drops of almond extract

15ml/1 tbsp milk
15ml/1 tbsp glycerine

FOR THE DECORATION
90ml/6 tbsp sieved (strained) apricot glaze
700g/1lb 9oz almond paste
1kg/2¼lb sugarpaste icing
paste food colourings, such as yellow, pink
   and blue

1 Preheat the oven to 160°C/325°F/Gas 3. Grease and line the base and sides of a 20cm/8in square cake tin (pan).

2 Sift the flour, baking powder and almonds into a large bowl. Add the margarine, caster sugar, eggs, almond extract, milk and glycerine and beat for about 2 minutes with an electric mixer until smooth.

3 Spoon into the tin and smooth level. Bake for 50 minutes to 1 hour, or until well risen, golden and firm in the middle.

4 Cool in the tin for 5 minutes, then turn out to cool on a wire rack.

5 When cold, remove the lining paper. Brush the cake with apricot glaze. Roll out the almond paste large enough to cover the cake. Lift on to the cake, smooth down the sides and trim. Set aside for 24 hours.

6 Colour half of the sugarpaste pale yellow and roll out to a square large enough to cover the cake. Brush the cake with a little cold boiled water, then lift the icing on to the cake and smooth down. Trim the edges neatly.

7 Colour half of the remaining sugarpaste blue and the rest pink.

8 Roll out the pink icing and cut four strips 4 × 20cm/1½ × 8in and eight strips 4 × 10cm/1½ × 4in.

9 Roll out the blue icing and cut four strips 2.5 × 20cm/1 × 8in and eight strips 2.5 × 10cm/1 × 4in. Centre matching length blue strips on top of the pink strips. Using a little water, stick the longer lengths to the cake top in a cross.

10 Form loops with four shorter strips. Leave to dry out overnight over the handle of a wooden spoon. Trim the ends of the remaining strips and stick to the cake top like ribbons. Stick the loops in place. Stamp the leftover icing into small shapes and use to decorate the cake.

Nutritional information per portion: Energy 483kcal/2024kJ; Protein 4.2g; Carbohydrate 63.6g, of which sugars 49.6g; Fat 25.4g, of which saturates 15.3g; Cholesterol 124mg; Calcium 105mg; Fibre 0.6g; Sodium 265mg.

Easter simnel cake

This cake is traditionally served at Easter. The marzipan balls on top represent the 11 faithful apostles. It is also sometimes made for Mothering Sunday, when the almond paste top is decorated with fresh or crystallized spring flowers.

SERVES 8–10

175g/6oz/¾ cup butter, plus extra
    for greasing
175g/6oz/¾ cup soft brown sugar
3 large (US extra large) eggs, beaten
225g/8oz/2 cups plain (all-purpose) flour
2.5ml/½ tsp ground cinnamon
2.5ml/½ tsp freshly grated nutmeg
450g/15oz/3 cups total weight currants,
    sultanas (golden raisins) and raisins

85g/3oz/scant ½ cup glacé (candied)
    cherries, quartered
85g/3oz/scant ½ cup chopped mixed
    (candied) peel,
grated rind of 1 large lemon
450g/1lb almond paste
icing (confectioners') sugar, for dusting
1 egg white, lightly beaten

1 Preheat the oven to 160°C/325°F/ Gas 3. Grease and line an 18cm/7in round cake tin (pan).

2 In a bowl, beat the butter and sugar, then the eggs. Fold in the flour, spices, dried fruits, cherries, mixed peel and the lemon rind.

3 Roll half the almond paste to a 16cm/6¼in circle on a surface dusted with icing sugar.

4 Spoon half the cake batter into the prepared tin. Put the circle of almond paste on top of the mixture. Spoon the remaining cake mixture on top of the almond paste and level the surface. Bake for 1 hour.

5 Reduce the temperature to 150°C/300°F/Gas 2 and bake for 2 more hours. Leave to cool in the tin.

6 Brush the cake with egg white. and use the remaining almond paste to cover the cake. Roll the remaining paste into 11 balls and attach with egg white. Brush the top with more egg white and grill (broil) until lightly browned.

Nutritional information per portion: Energy 810kcal/ 3416kJ; Protein 10.4g; Carbohydrate 132g, of which sugars 111g; Fat 30.4g, of which saturates 13.2g; Cholesterol 144mg; Calcium 156mg; Fibre 33g; Sodium 208mg.

Easy birthday cake

Make celebrating a birthday simple with this scrumptious caramel cake, which can be decorated to make it suitable for either children or adults. The fudgy icing is made in a pan then swirled over the top and sides of the cake in moments – it really couldn't be easier.

SERVES 10–12

175g/6oz/³⁄₄ cup soft tub margarine,
   plus extra for greasing
225g/8oz/2 cups self-raising
   (self-rising) flour
2.5ml/¹⁄₂ tsp baking powder
225g/8oz/1 cup soft light brown sugar
3 eggs, beaten
30ml/2 tbsp golden (light corn) syrup
60ml/4 tbsp milk
5ml/1 tbsp vanilla extract

FOR THE CARAMEL ICING

115g/4oz/¹⁄₂ cup unsalted butter
225g/8oz/1 cup soft light brown sugar
60ml/4 tbsp milk
115g/4oz/1 cup icing
   (confectioners') sugar
sweets (candies) and candles, to decorate

1 Preheat the oven to 180°C/350°F/ Gas 4. Grease and line the bases of two 20cm/8in shallow round cake tins (pans) with baking parchment.

2 Sift the flour and baking powder into a large bowl, then add the margarine, soft light brown sugar, eggs, syrup, milk and vanilla extract. Beat with an electric mixer for about 2 minutes, or until smooth, then divide between the tins.

3 Bake for 30 minutes, or until firm to the touch. Allow to cool for 5 minutes, then turn out on a wire rack. Remove the lining paper.

4 To make the icing, melt the butter in a pan, add the brown sugar and milk, stir then bring to the boil. Reduce the heat, simmer for about 2 minutes, then pour into a bowl and leave to cool. When cold, beat in the icing sugar.

5 Swirl the icing over the top and sides of the cake. Decorate with sweets and candles or use chocolate buttons and broken flaked chocolate, as desired.

6 The undecorated cake keeps for 4 days in an airtight tin.

Nutritional information per portion: Energy 570kcal/ 2408kJ; Protein 3.8g; Carbohydrate 108.8g, of which sugars 95.1g; Fat 16.3g, of which saturates 9.6g; Cholesterol 18mg; Calcium 64mg; Fibre 0.6g; Sodium 293mg.

Mother's Day cake

Almonds, orange and vanilla give this special cake its distinctive flavour, which can be further enhanced by drizzling over a little orange liqueur.

SERVES 12

200g/7oz/scant 1 cup butter, softened, plus extra for greasing

2 small oranges

100g/3³⁄₄oz/scant 1 cup toasted flaked (sliced) almonds

200g/7oz/1 cup soft light brown sugar

4 eggs, beaten

5ml/1 tsp vanilla extract

175g/6oz/1¹⁄₂ cups self-raising (self-rising) flour

40g/1³⁄₄oz/generous ¹⁄₄ cup natural icing (confectioners') sugar, plus extra dusting

5ml/1 tbsp orange liqueur (optional)

FOR THE DECORATION

¹⁄₂ quantity buttercream icing, see page 218

675g/1¹⁄₂lb sugarpaste

Materials: 1.5m/1yd fancy ribbon; bought sugarpaste or silk flowers

1 Preheat the oven to 180°C/350°F/Gas 4. Grease and line a 20cm/8in round springform cake tin (pan) with baking parchment.

2 Peel the oranges in strips, then put in a food processor. Process for a few seconds until the peel forms a fine powder, then put into a bowl. Process the almonds until fine, then mix with the powdered rind.

3 Beat the butter and sugar together until light and fluffy. Whisk in the eggs gradually, adding 5ml/1 tsp flour with each addition to prevent the mixture from curdling. Fold in the remaining flour with the almond and rind mixture until smooth, then spoon into the tin. Bake for about 40 minutes, or until golden and firm.

4 Meanwhile, squeeze the juice from 1 orange and put in a small pan with the icing sugar and 3 tbsp/45ml cold water, and simmer for 10 minutes, or until syrupy. Add the orange liqueur, if using.

5 Remove the paper. Prick the top of the cake and spoon the syrup over, then leave to cool in the tin. Cut the cake in half horizontally. Spread one cut cake side with buttercream icing. Sandwich the other layer on top and spread thinly all over with buttercream.

6 Roll out the sugarpaste on a surface dusted with icing sugar and use to cover the cake. Smooth over the cake. Trim the base and tie a ribbon around the sides. Top with sugarpaste or silk flowers.

Nutritional information per portion: Energy 573kcal/2419kJ; Protein 10.2g; Carbohydrate 98.7g, of which sugars 95.6g; Fat 18g, of which saturates 1.9g; Cholesterol 73mg; Calcium 138mg; Fibre 2.4g; Sodium 52mg.

Celebratory anniversary cake

Sugarpaste makes a smooth finish for a cake and can also be used to mould these delicate arum lilies. Colour the centre of the lilies silver to indicate 25 years of marriage or gold for 50 years.

SERVES 30

175g/6oz/³⁄₄ cup butter, plus extra
   for greasing
450g/1lb/2²⁄₃ cups mixed dried fruit
50g/2oz/¹⁄₄ cup glacé (candied)
   cherries, chopped
150g/5oz/generous ¹⁄₂ cup ready-to-eat
   dried apricots, chopped
115g/4oz/scant 1 cup dried, stoned (pitted)
   dates, chopped
165g/5¹⁄₂oz/scant 1¹⁄₂ cups dried, stoned
   (pitted) prunes, chopped
50g/2oz/¹⁄₄ cup dried peaches, chopped
175g/6oz/³⁄₄ cup muscovado
   (molasses) sugar
2 oranges and 1 lemon

15ml/1 tbsp mixed (apple pie) spice
15ml/1 tbsp treacle (molasses)
4 eggs, beaten
250g/9oz/2¹⁄₄ cups plain (all-purpose) flour
5ml/1 tsp baking powder

FOR THE DECORATION
60ml/4 tbsp apricot glaze
900g/2lb almond paste
1.2kg/2¹⁄₂lb ivory-coloured sugarpaste
Materials: 8 strands of green floristry wire;
   gold or silver food colouring or dusting
   powder; 10 strands of bear grass;
   1.5m/1³⁄₄yd silver or gold fine net ribbon

1 Put the butter in a large, heavy pan and add the dried fruits and the muscovado sugar. Grate in the rind from one orange and the lemon. Squeeze in the juice from both oranges and the lemon with 75ml/2¹⁄₂fl oz/¹⁄₃ cup water. Heat gently, stirring, for 10 minutes, or until the butter melts and the sugar dissolves. Pour into a large bowl, stir in the mixed spice and treacle, and leave to stand overnight.

2 Preheat the oven to 160°C/325°F/Gas 3. Grease and triple-line a 20cm/8in square tin (pan) or a 23cm/9in round cake tin, and wrap four layers of newspaper around the sides.

3 Add the eggs to the fruit mixture, then sift in the flour and baking powder. Mix until smooth. Pour into the prepared tin and level the top. Cover with two layers of baking parchment to prevent over-browning. Bake for 2 hours, then lower the temperature to 150°C/300°F/Gas 2 and bake for a further 1³⁄₄ –2 hours.

4 Test with a skewer inserted into the centre; it will come out clean when the cake is cooked. Cool in the tin, then turn out and wrap in foil to mature for 2–3 months. Remove the lining paper. To decorate the cake, brush with the apricot glaze and cover with almond paste. Leave for 24 hours.

5 Roll out the sugarpaste icing to a square large enough to cover the cake. Brush the cake with water, place the sugarpaste on the cake, smooth over the top and sides, and trim. Make a small flat loop at the top of each piece of floristry wire to help the sugarpaste adhere to the wire. Re-roll the sugarpaste scraps to make 8 thin rolls and wrap these around the floristry wires. Dry for 24 hours.

6 Roll out the remaining sugarpaste and cut into rectangles 10 × 9cm/4 × 3in. Wrap each into a cone around the centre, leaving a pointed tip. Flute out the edges. Dry upside down in egg boxes for 24 hours. Paint the tips of the lily stamens silver or gold. Arrange lilies with strands of bear grass and tie this with a ribbon to secure. Arrange on the cake. Trim the sides with ribbon.

Nutritional information per portion: Energy 224kcal/936kJ; Protein 2.4g; Carbohydrate 26.7g, of which sugars 20.5g; Fat 12.6g, of which saturates 7.6g; Cholesterol 17mg; Calcium 26mg; Fibre 0.7g; Sodium 168mg.

Rose-petal wedding cake

This special two-tiered cake looks very dainty with its pink and white glossy buttercream icing decorated with rose petals. You can bake the cake bases a day or two before you need them, then decorate them with the simple icing on the day.

SERVES 18

FOR THE SMALL CAKE
115g/4oz/¹/₂ cup butter, softened, plus
    extra for greasing
115/4oz/1 cup self-raising (self-rising) flour
2.5ml/¹/₂ tsp baking powder
115g/4oz/generous ¹/₂ cup natural caster
    (superfine) sugar
2 eggs, beaten
15ml/1 tbsp milk
a few drops of rose water

FOR THE LARGE CAKE
350g/12oz/1¹/₂ cups butter, softened, plus
    extra for greasing
350g/12oz/3 cups self-raising
    (self-rising) flour
5ml/1 tsp baking powder

350g/12oz/1¹/₂ cups natural caster
    (superfine) sugar
6 eggs, beaten
30ml/2 tbsp milk
a few drops of rose water

FOR THE DECORATION
4 egg whites
275g/10oz/2¹/₂ cups icing
    (confectioners') sugar
275g/10 oz/1¹/₄ cups unsalted
    butter, beaten
a few drops of rose water
pink food colouring
120ml/4fl oz/¹/₂ cup apricot jam
crystallized rose petals

1 Make and bake the two cakes separately. Preheat the oven to 160°C/ 325°F/Gas 3. Grease and line a 15cm/6in round deep cake tin (pan) with baking parchment.

2 To make the small cake, sift the flour and baking powder into a bowl. Add the sugar, butter, eggs, milk and rose water. Beat for 2 minutes, until smooth. Spoon into the cake tin and smooth the top. Bake for 30–40 minutes, until firm and golden. Turn out to cool on a wire rack. Repeat steps 1–3 to make the large cake, using a 25cm/10in round cake tin. Bake for 1 hour 10 minutes.

3 Whisk the egg whites and icing sugar in a bowl set over a pan of hot water until the beaters leave a trail when lifted. Remove from the heat. Continue whisking until soft peaks form. Cool slightly, then beat into the softened butter and rose water. Put 45ml/3 tbsp of the mixture into a piping (pastry) bag and snip a tiny hole off the end.

4 Colour one-third of the remaining icing pale pink and put 60ml/4 tbsp in another paper icing bag, then snip off the end. Remove the paper linings. Slice each cake in half horizontally.

5 Sandwich together with apricot jam. Cover the small cake with pink icing and smooth flat. Cover the large cake with white icing and smooth it flat. Using a metal spatula, put the small cake on top of the large one. Remove the spatula carefully to avoid spreading cake crumbs.

6 Pipe tiny beads around the base of each cake. Sprinkle crystallized rose petals over the cakes and around the base before serving.

Nutritional information per portion: Energy 253kcal/1071kJ; Protein 2.5g; Carbohydrate 48.8g, of which sugars 44.6g; Fat 5.5g, of which saturates 1.1g; Cholesterol 17mg; Calcium 49mg; Fibre 0.9g; Sodium 63mg.

Traditional Christmas cake

Make this cake a few weeks before Christmas. Once or twice during this time, pierce the cake with a skewer and spoon over 30–45ml/2–3 tbsp brandy to make it beautifully moist and rich.

SERVES 20

225g/8oz/1¹/₃ cups sultanas (golden raisins)

225g/8oz/1 cup currants

225g/8oz/1¹/₃ cups raisins

115g/4oz/¹/₂ cup prunes, stoned (pitted) and chopped

50g/2oz/¹/₄ cup glacé (candied) cherries, halved

50g/2oz/¹/₃ cup chopped mixed (candied) peel,

45ml/3 tbsp brandy or sherry

225g/8oz/1 cup butter, plus extra for greasing

225g/8oz/2 cups plain (all-purpose) flour

pinch of salt

2.5ml/¹/₂ tsp ground cinnamon

2.5ml/¹/₂ tsp freshly grated nutmeg

15ml/1 tbsp unsweetened cocoa powder

225g/8oz/1 cup soft dark brown sugar

4 large (US extra large) eggs

finely grated rind of 1 orange or 1 lemon

50g/2oz/¹/₂ cup ground almonds

50g/2oz/¹/₂ cup chopped almonds

FOR THE DECORATION

60ml/4 tbsp apricot jam

icing (confectioners') sugar for dusting

450g/1lb almond paste, see page 220

30ml/2 tbsp Kirsch or brandy

450g/1lb white sugarpaste icing, see page 221

225g/8oz royal icing, see page 221

Materials: ribbon

1 The day before you want to bake the cake, put all the dried fruit in a large bowl. Pour in the brandy or sherry, cover with clear film (plastic wrap) and leave overnight.

2 Preheat the oven to 170°C/325°F/Gas 3. Grease and line the base and sides of a 20cm/8in round cake tin (pan) with a double thickness of baking parchment.

3 Sift together the flour, salt, spices and cocoa powder into a large bowl. In a large bowl, beat the butter and sugar together until light and fluffy, then beat in each egg. Mix in the citrus rind, both almonds, dried fruits (with any liquid) and the flour mixture. Spoon into the prepared tin and smooth the surface level. Give the cake tin a gentle tap on the work surface to settle the batter and disperse any air bubbles. Bake for 3 hours, or until a skewer inserted into the centre comes out clean.

4 Leave the cake to cool in the tin for an hour. Turn the cake out on to a wire rack, but leave the paper on, as it will help to keep the cake moist during storage. When the cake is cold, wrap it tightly in foil and store in a cool place until ready to decorate.

5 Put the apricot jam in a pan and heat to warm, then sieve (strain) it to make a glaze. Remove the lining paper and centre the cake on a cake board. Brush the cake with hot jam.

6 Dust the work surface with icing sugar. Roll out the almond paste. Pick the almond paste up on the rolling pin and fit over the surface. Smooth out any air bubbles. Trim away any excess. Brush with 30ml/2 tbsp Kirsch. Roll out the sugarpaste and cover the cake. Trim the excess.

7 Roll out sugarpaste trimmings and stamp out decorations. Lift with a palette knife, then stick down with a little royal icing. Use a star nozzle in a piping (pastry) bag and one-third fill it with royal icing. Pipe rosettes around the base of the cake. Leave to dry. Tie a ribbon around the sides of the cake.

Nutritional information per portion: Energy 6637kcal/28042kJ; Protein 60.6g; Carbohydrate 1245.8g, of which sugars 1129.2g; Fat 166.7g, of which saturates 85.9g; Cholesterol 940mg; Calcium 1515mg; Fibre 31.1g; Sodium 1896mg.

Festive Yule log

The chocolate-covered Yule log has its origins in France. It makes a good alternative for those who don't like the traditional rich fruit cake, or it can be served during the Christmas holidays as a dessert with a fresh fruit compote. Eat this fresh or freeze it, unfilled, for two months.

SERVES 8

butter, for greasing
90g/3½oz/¾ cup self-raising
    (self-rising) flour
30ml/2 tbsp unsweetened cocoa powder
pinch of salt
4 eggs
115g/4oz/generous ½ cup golden caster
    (superfine) sugar, plus extra for dusting

FOR THE FILLING AND ICING

150ml/¼ pint/⅔ cup double (heavy) cream
50g/2oz plain (semisweet) chocolate
30ml/2 tbsp unsweetened cocoa powder
15ml/2 tbsp boiling water
115g/4oz/½ cup unsalted butter, softened
225g/8oz/2 cups natural icing
    (confectioners') sugar, sifted, plus extra
    for dusting
almond paste or chocolate holly leaves,
    to decorate

1 Preheat the oven to 220°C/425°F/Gas 7. Grease and line a 33 × 23cm/ 13 × 9in Swiss roll tin (jelly roll pan).

2 Sift the flour, cocoa and salt into a bowl.

3 Put the eggs and sugar into a large heatproof bowl and place this over a pan of hot water. Whisk for 10 minutes, or until the mixture is thick. Remove the bowl from the water and whisk until the mixture is thick and pale, and leaves a trail when the beaters are lifted away.

4 Using a large metal spoon, gently fold in half the flour and cocoa using a figure-of-eight movement. Fold in the remaining flour with 15ml/1 tbsp cold water. Pour the mixture into the prepared tin and smooth level.

5 Bake for 10 minutes, or until springy to the touch. Sprinkle a sheet of baking parchment with caster sugar and place this on a clean dish towel.

6 Turn the hot sponge out on to the paper.

7 Peel away the lining paper. Trim away the crusty sponge edges. Using the dish towel, roll up the sponge loosely, with the paper inside, then leave to cool on a wire rack.

8 Carefully unwrap the cold sponge cake and remove the paper. Whip the cream until stiff, spread over the sponge, then roll up and chill until needed.

9 Melt the chocolate in a heatproof bowl over a pan of gently simmering water, then leave to cool.

10 Dissolve the cocoa in the boiling water, stir until blended, then leave to cool.

11 Beat the butter until fluffy, then beat in the icing sugar and cooled cocoa with the melted chocolate.

12 Put the cake on a long serving dish. Spread the chocolate icing over the top and sides of the cake with a metal spatula, in deep swirls and ridges.

13 Decorate the top with almond paste or chocolate holly leaves and dust very lightly with a sprinkle of icing sugar before serving.

COOK'S TIP

The sponge mixture for a Swiss roll is rolled up while it is still hot, to help prevent it cracking.

Nutritional information per portion: Energy 478kcal/ 2003kJ; Protein 7.1g; Carbohydrate 55.4g, of which sugars 44.1g; Fat 26.1g, of which saturates 15g; Cholesterol 130mg; Calcium 75mg; Fibre 1.4g; Sodium 47mg.

White Christmas cake

This light and zesty cake makes a refreshing change to a traditional heavy fruit cake. Make the moist sponge bases a day ahead, or bake and freeze them to keep life simple over the holiday, so that all you have to do is add the very easy filling and decoration. Eat on the day it is made.

SERVES 12

225g/8oz/1 cup unsalted butter, softened,
   plus extra for greasing
finely grated rind and juice of 2 limes
75g/3oz block creamed coconut, grated or
   150ml coconut cream
225g/8oz/generous 1 cup caster
   (superfine) sugar
4 large (US extra large) eggs
225g/8oz/2 cups self-raising
   (self-rising) flour

FOR THE FILLING AND DECORATION

200g/7oz/scant ³/₄ cup lemon curd
225g/8oz/1 cup cream cheese
75g/3oz/6 tbsp unsalted butter
275g/10oz/2¹/₂ cups icing
   (confectioners') sugar
finely grated rind of 1 lime
175g/6oz/2 cups shredded coconut
crystallized sprigs of bay leaf, rosemary and
   cranberries, or silver Christmas baubles or
   snowflake ornaments, to decorate

1 Preheat the oven to 180°C/350°F/Gas 4. Grease and line two 20cm/8in round cake tins (pans).

2 Put the lime juice and 30ml/2 tbsp water in a small pan with the creamed coconut and heat gently to dissolve, then cool.

3 Put the lime rind, butter, sugar, eggs, flour and cooled coconut mixture into a bowl and whisk for 2–3 minutes, or until smooth and soft. Divide the batter equally between the cake tins and smooth the tops level. Bake for 20–25 minutes, or until golden and risen, and firm to the touch in the centre. Cool in the tin for 5 minutes, then turn out to cool on a wire rack and peel away the lining papers.

4 Cut each cake in half horizontally with a sharp knife, then sandwich each together with lemon curd. Put one cake on a plate, spread the top with the remaining lemon curd and sandwich together.

5 To make the coating, put the cream cheese, butter, icing sugar and lime rind in a bowl and beat until smooth. Spread the coating over the top and sides of the cake. Sprinkle the coconut over the top and pat on to the sides, then tidy the base. Decorate the cake with rosemary and cranberries.

Nutritional information per portion: Energy 698Kcal/2912kJ; Protein 8.9g; Carbohydrate 63g, of which sugars 51.8g; Fat 47.5g, of which saturates 34.7g; Cholesterol 193mg; Calcium 78mg; Fibre 6.4g; Sodium 188mg.

Loaf Cakes and Tray Bakes

These bakes belong to the more informal side of cake making. Traybakes are simple to make and as they can be packed easily and feed many people, they are ideal for cake stalls or picnics or to take to coffee mornings. Vanilla Streusel Bars or Mint Choc Brownies are sure to be popular. The perfect tea time treat, loaf cakes can be eaten as they are, buttered or toasted. Banana Bread, and Apricot and Lemon Loaf are two delicious examples.

Pineapple and carrot cake

This is one of the most irresistible cakes ever invented. The poppy seeds and walnut pieces add crunch, and a tangy citrus mascarpone icing makes a delicious topping.

SERVES 10–12

115g/4oz/½ cup butter, melted and
   cooled, plus extra for greasing
250g/9oz/2¼ cups plain
   (all-purpose) flour
10ml/2 tsp baking powder
5ml/1 tsp bicarbonate of soda (baking soda)
pinch of salt
5ml/1 tsp ground cinnamon
45ml/3 tbsp poppy seeds
225g/8oz/1 cup soft light brown sugar
3 eggs, beaten
finely grated rind of 1 orange
225g/8oz raw carrots, finely grated
75g/3oz fresh or canned pineapple,
   drained and finely chopped
75g/3oz/¾ cup walnut pieces

FOR THE ICING

150g/5oz/scant ¾ cup mascarpone
30ml/2 tbsp icing (confectioners') sugar
finely grated rind of 1 orange

1 Preheat the oven to 180°C/350°F/Gas 4. Grease and line a 900g/2lb loaf tin (pan) with baking parchment.

2 Sift the flour, baking powder, bicarbonate of soda, salt and cinnamon into a bowl. Stir in the poppy seeds.

3 In another large bowl, put the sugar, eggs and orange rind. Beat together until smooth and frothy. Squeeze the excess moisture from the carrots and stir them into the egg mixture with the pineapple and walnut pieces.

4 Stir the flour into the egg mixture, then gently fold in the melted butter. Spoon the batter into the prepared tin and smooth the top level. Bake for 1–1¼ hours, or until risen and golden. Leave to cool for 10 minutes, then turn out on a wire rack. Remove the paper when cold.

5 To make the icing, beat the mascarpone with the icing sugar and orange rind. Spread thickly over the top of the cake.

Nutritional information per portion: Energy 400kcal/1668kJ; Protein 4.2g; Carbohydrate 39.1g, of which sugars 29.9g; Fat 26.3g, of which saturates 7.2g; Cholesterol 55mg; Calcium 62mg; Fibre 1g; Sodium 67mg.

Sour cherry coffee loaf

Dried sour cherries have a concentrated fruit flavour that makes them ideal for adding to cakes. Here they are partnered with strong brewed coffee, both in the cake and in the delicious icing.

SERVES 8–10

175g/6oz/³⁄4 cup butter, softened, plus extra for greasing
175g/6oz/scant 1 cup golden caster (superfine) sugar
5ml/1 tsp vanilla extract
2 eggs, lightly beaten
225g/8oz/2 cups plain (all-purpose) flour
1.5ml/¹⁄4 tsp baking powder
75ml/5 tbsp strong brewed instant coffee
175g/6oz/1 cup dried sour cherries

FOR THE ICING

50g/2oz/¹⁄2 cup icing (confectioners') sugar, sifted
20ml/4 tsp strong brewed instant coffee

1 Preheat the oven to 180°C/350°F/Gas 4. Grease and line a 900g/2lb loaf tin (pan).

2 In a large bowl, cream the butter, sugar and vanilla extract until light and fluffy. Gradually add the eggs, beating well after each addition. Add a teaspoon of flour if the mixture curdles. Sift the flour and baking powder together over the bowl. Fold into the mixture using a metal spoon, then fold in the coffee and two-thirds of the sour cherries.

3 Spoon the mixture into the prepared tin and smooth the top level. Bake for 1¼ hours, or until firm to the touch. Cool in the tin for 5 minutes, then carefully turn the loaf out on to a wire rack to cool. Remove the lining paper.

4 To make the icing, mix together the icing sugar and coffee, and the remaining cherries. Spoon over the top and sides. Leave to set before slicing.

Nutritional information per portion: Energy 307kcal/1283kJ; Protein 2.1g; Carbohydrate 33.1g, of which sugars 33.1g; Fat 19.4g, of which saturates 11.8g; Cholesterol 94mg; Calcium 30mg; Fibre 0.3g; Sodium 152mg.

Chocolate-chip marzipan loaf

Here, almond paste is chopped into chunks and stirred into the batter with chocolate chips. When baked, the marzipan is wonderfully creamy – a surprise inside an ordinary-looking cake.

SERVES 10

115g/4oz/¹⁄₂ cup unsalted butter, softened, plus extra for greasing

150g/5oz/generous ¹⁄₂ cup light muscovado (brown) sugar

2 eggs

45ml/3 tbsp unsweetened cocoa powder

150g/5oz/1¹⁄₄ cups self-raising (self-rising) flour

130g/4¹⁄₂oz almond paste

60ml/4 tbsp plain (semisweet) chocolate chips

1 Preheat the oven to 180°C/350°F/Gas 4. Grease and line a 900g/2lb loaf tin (pan) with baking parchment.

2 In a bowl, beat the butter and sugar together until light and fluffy, then beat in the eggs one at a time. Sift the cocoa and flour over the mixture and fold in evenly.

3 Chop the almond paste into small pieces. Transfer to a bowl and mix with the chocolate chips. Set aside about 60ml/4 tbsp of mixed almond paste and chocolate chips and fold the rest evenly into the cake mixture.

4 Spoon the batter into the prepared tin, level the top and sprinkle with the reserved almond paste and chocolate chips.

5 Bake for 45–50 minutes, or until the loaf is risen and firm. Cool for a few minutes in the tin, then turn out and leave to go cold. Remove the paper.

Nutritional information per portion: Energy 291kcal/1224kJ; Protein 4.6g; Carbohydrate 36.8g, of which sugars 24.8g; Fat 15g, of which saturates 8g; Cholesterol 62.9mg; Calcium 51mg; Fibre 1.4g; Sodium 130mg.

Gingerbread

Cinnamon as well as ginger gives gingerbread its warm flavouring. Treacle and golden syrup are the essential ingredients to ensure the finished cake is soft and sticky.

SERVES 8–10

75g/3oz/6 tbsp butter, plus extra
   for greasing
115g/4oz/¹/₂ cup soft light brown sugar
75g/3oz/¹/₄ cup golden (light corn) syrup
75g/3oz/¹/₄ cup treacle (molasses)
105ml/7 tbsp milk
1 egg, beaten
175g/6oz/1¹/₂ cups plain
   (all-purpose) flour
50g/2oz/¹/₂ cup gram flour
pinch of salt
10ml/2 tsp ground ginger
5ml/1 tsp ground cinnamon
7.5ml/1¹/₂ tsp baking powder

1 Preheat the oven to 160°C/325°F/Gas 3. Grease and line a 900g/2lb loaf tin (pan) with baking parchment.

2 Put the sugar, butter, golden syrup and treacle in a pan and heat gently until melted, stirring occasionally. Remove from the heat. Cool slightly. Mix in the milk and egg.

3 Sift the flours, salt, spices and baking powder into a large bowl. Make a well in the centre and pour in the liquid mixture. Beat well. Pour the batter into the tin. Bake for 1–1¹/₄ hours, or until firm.

4 Leave in the tin for about 5 minutes, then turn out on to a wire rack to go cold. Peel off the lining paper before slicing.

Nutritional information per portion: Energy 191kcal/802kJ; Protein 1.6g; Carbohydrate 24.7g, of which sugars 24.6g; Fat 10.3g, of which saturates 6.3g; Cholesterol 45mg; Calcium 128mg; Fibre 0g; Sodium 116mg.

Banana bread

When you have some bananas that have become overripe in the fruit bowl, use them for this quick recipe. They need to be very ripe and will give the bread a lovely sweetness and fragrance.

SERVES 8–10

115g/4oz/½ cup butter, plus extra
   for greasing
5ml/1 tsp bicarbonate of soda
   (baking soda)
225g/8oz/2 cups wholemeal
   (whole-wheat) flour
2 eggs, beaten
3 very ripe bananas
30–45ml/2–3 tbsp coconut milk

1 Preheat the oven to 180°C/350°F/Gas 4. Grease and line a 900g/2lb loaf tin (pan) with baking parchment.

2 In a large bowl, cream the butter until it is fluffy.

3 Sift the bicarbonate of soda with the flour, then add to the butter, alternating with the eggs.

4 Peel the bananas and slice them on to a plate. Mash them well, using the back of a fork, then stir them into the cake mixture. Mix in the coconut milk and stir together.

5 Spoon the batter into the tin and smooth the top level. Bake for 1¼ hours, or until golden and firm to the touch. Cool on a wire rack. Remove the lining paper.

Nutritional information per portion: Energy 226kcal/954kJ; Protein 5.1g; Carbohydrate 37.2g, of which sugars 19.5g; Fat 73.g, of which saturates 3.8g; Cholesterol 51mg; Calcium 46mg; Fibre 1.8g; Sodium 55mg.

Apricot and lemon loaf

This lovely cake has apricots and nuts in the crumb itself, and is topped with a crunchy layer of almonds and pistachio nuts. After baking it is soaked in a tangy lemon syrup to keep it moist.

SERVES 8–10

175g/6oz/³/₄ cup butter, softened, plus extra for greasing
175g/6oz/1¹/₂ cups self-raising (self-rising) flour, sifted
2.5ml/¹/₂ tsp baking powder
175g/6oz/scant 1 cup caster (superfine) sugar
3 eggs, lightly beaten
finely grated rind of 1 lemon
175g/6oz/1¹/₂ cups ready-to-eat dried apricots, finely chopped
75g/3oz/³/₄ cup ground almonds
40g/1¹/₂oz/¹/₃ cup pistachio nuts, chopped
50g/2oz/¹/₂ cup flaked almonds
15g/¹/₂oz/2 tbsp whole pistachio nuts

FOR THE SYRUP
freshly squeezed juice of 1 lemon
45ml/3 tbsp caster (superfine) sugar

1 Preheat the oven to 180°C/350°F/Gas 4. Grease and line a 900g/2lb loaf tin (pan) with baking parchment.

2 Put the butter, flour and baking powder into a large bowl, then add the sugar, eggs and lemon rind. Beat for 1–2 minutes, or until smooth and glossy. Stir in the apricots, ground almonds and the chopped pistachio nuts.

3 Spoon the batter into the tin and smooth the surface. Sprinkle with the flaked almonds and whole pistachio nuts. Bake for 1¼ hours, or until a skewer inserted into the centre comes out clean. Check the cake after about 45 minutes and cover with a piece of foil once the top is nicely brown. Leave to cool in the tin.

4 To make the syrup, put the lemon juice and sugar into a pan and heat gently, stirring occasionally, until the sugar has dissolved. Spoon the syrup over the cake. When the cake is cold, turn it out and peel off the lining paper.

Nutritional information per portion: Energy 436kcal/1822kJ; Protein 8.1g; Carbohydrate 44.3g, of which sugars 30.5g; Fat 26.4g, of which saturates 10.5g; Cholesterol 94mg; Calcium 96mg; Fibre 2.9g; Sodium 162mg.

Marmalade teabread

Chunky orange marmalade adds a touch of citrus zest to this spicy teabread. It is so quick and easy to make and perfect for serving with a cup of tea. Keep this cake for up to three days in an airtight container, or freeze it for up to two months wrapped in foil.

SERVES 6–8

100g/3¾oz/7 tbsp butter, diced, plus
    extra for greasing
200g/7oz/1¾ cups plain
    (all-purpose) flour
5ml/1 tsp baking powder
6.25ml/1¼ tsp ground cinnamon
50g/2oz/¼ cup soft light brown sugar
1 egg, lightly beaten
60ml/4 tbsp chunky orange marmalade
about 45ml/3 tbsp milk
60ml/4 tbsp glacé icing, to decorate
shreds of orange and lemon rind,
    to decorate

1 Preheat the oven to 160°C/325°F/Gas 3. Grease and line a 450g/1lb loaf tin (pan) with baking parchment.

2 Sift the flour, baking powder and cinnamon into a mixing bowl. Add the butter and rub in with your fingertips until the mixture resembles fine crumbs. Stir in the sugar.

3 In a bowl, mix the egg with the marmalade and most of the milk. Stir the milk mixture into the flour, adding more milk if necessary to give a soft, dropping consistency. Spoon into the prepared tin and level the top. Bake for 1¼ hours, or until the cake is firm to the touch and cooked through.

4 Leave to stand in the tin for 5 minutes, then turn out to cool on a wire rack. Peel off the lining paper. Drizzle the glacé icing over the top of the cake and decorate with shreds of orange and lemon rind.

Nutritional information per portion: Energy 287kcal/1206kJ; Protein 8.3g; Carbohydrate 34.8g, of which sugars 9.3g; Fat 13.7g, of which saturates 8.1g; Cholesterol 63mg; Calcium 68mg; Fibre 1g; Sodium 554mg.

Coconut cake

Sour cream and desiccated coconut make this quick and easy cake very moist, with a full flavour that is lifted by a delicious lemony tang. This cake keeps for eight days in an airtight container.

SERVES 8–10

115g/4oz/1 cup butter, softened, plus
  extra for greasing
115g/4oz/generous ½ cup caster
  (superfine) sugar
2 large (US extra large) eggs, beaten
115g/4oz/generous 1 cup desiccated (dry
  unsweetened shredded) coconut
115g/4oz/1 cup self-raising
  (self-rising) flour
75ml/5 tbsp sour cream or natural
  (plain) yogurt
15ml/1 tbsp finely grated lemon rind

1 Preheat the oven to 180°C/350°F/Gas 4. Grease and line a 900g/2lb loaf tin (pan) with baking parchment.

2 In a large bowl, beat the butter and sugar together until pale and fluffy, then add the eggs in batches, beating well after each addition.

3 Add the coconut, flour, sour cream and lemon rind, and beat together until smooth.

4 Spoon into the tin. Bake for 50 minutes, or until a skewer inserted into the centre comes out clean.

5 Cool in the tin for 5 minutes, then turn out on to a wire rack to go cold. Peel off the lining paper.

Nutritional information per portion: Energy 221kcal/924kJ; Protein 3g; Carbohydrate 27.8g, of which sugars 22.1g; Fat 11.6g, of which saturates 8.2g; Cholesterol 61mg; Calcium 31mg; Fibre 1.6g; Sodium 51mg.

Lemon and walnut teabread

The unusual combination of earthy walnuts and fresh zesty lemons works well here. Unusually for a teabread, whisked egg whites are added to the batter, making it light and airy. Keep for three days in an airtight container or freeze for two months wrapped in foil.

SERVES 8–10

115g/4oz/½ cup butter, softened, plus
    extra for greasing
100g/3¾oz/generous ½ cup caster
    (superfine) sugar
2 eggs, separated
grated rind of 2 lemons
30ml/2 tbsp lemon juice
200g/7oz/1¾ cups plain
    (all-purpose) flour
10ml/2 tsp baking powder
120ml/4fl oz/½ cup milk
50g/2oz/½ cup walnuts, chopped
pinch of salt

1 Preheat the oven to 180°C/350°F/ Gas 4. Grease and line a 900g/ 2lb loaf tin (pan) with baking parchment.

2 Beat the butter with the sugar. Beat in the egg yolks, lemon rind and juice. Set aside.

3 Sift the flour and baking powder over the butter mixture in batches, and stir well, alternating with the milk. Fold in the walnuts.

4 Put the egg whites into a clean, grease-free bowl and whisk until they form stiff peaks. Fold a large tablespoon of the egg whites into the walnut mixture to lighten it. Fold in the remaining egg whites until just blended.

5 Pour the batter into the tin and smooth the top level. Bake for 45–50 minutes, or until a skewer inserted into the centre comes out clean.

6 Leave to stand in the tin for 5 minutes then turn out on to a wire rack to go cold. Peel off the lining.

Nutritional information per portion: Energy 249kcal/ 1041kJ; Protein 4.5g; Carbohydrate 26.9g, of which sugars 10.4g; Fat 14.4g, of which saturates 6.7g; Cholesterol 63mg; Calcium 61mg; Fibre 0.8g; Sodium 90mg.

Raspberry and almond teabread

Fresh raspberries and almonds combine perfectly to flavour this mouthwatering loaf with its crunchy, toasted almond topping. Serve warm with a spoonful of crème fraîche for tea or to serve as a quick dessert. Eat this cake on the day it is made.

SERVES 6–8

90g/3½oz/7 tbsp butter, plus extra
   for greasing
175g/6oz/1½ cups self-raising (self-
   rising) flour
90g/3½oz/½ cup caster
   (superfine) sugar
40g/1½oz/scant ½ cup
   ground almonds
2 eggs, beaten
30ml/2 tbsp milk
115g/4oz/1 cup fresh raspberries or
   partly thawed frozen raspberries
30ml/2 tbsp toasted flaked
   (sliced) almonds

1 Preheat the oven to 180°C/
350°F/Gas 4. Grease and line
a 450g/1lb loaf tin (pan) with
baking parchment.

2 Sift the flour into a large bowl
or the bowl of a food processor.
Add the butter and rub in, or
process, until the mixture
resembles fine breadcrumbs.

3 Stir in the sugar and ground
almonds, then gradually mix
in the eggs and milk, and beat
until smooth.

4 Fold in the raspberries, being
careful not to crush them.

5 Spoon into the prepared tin and
sprinkle over the flaked almonds.

6 Bake for about 55 minutes, or
until a skewer inserted into the
centre comes out clean.

7 Cool the cake in the tin, then turn
out on to a wire rack to go cold.
Remove the lining paper.

Nutritional information per portion: Energy 215kcal/
902kJ; Protein 4.3g; Carbohydrate 24.1g, of which sugars
10.5g; Fat 12g, of which saturates 5.3g; Cholesterol
44mg; Calcium 59mg; Fibre 1.4g; Sodium 79mg.

Peanut butter teabread

Crunchy peanut butter gives this teabread a distinctive flavour and texture. It also adds protein to make it into a substantial snack. The salted peanuts contrast with the sweetness of the bread.

SERVES 10

50g/2oz/¼ cup butter, softened, plus
   extra for greasing
225g/8oz/2 cups plain (all-purpose) flour
7.5ml/1½ tsp baking powder
2.5ml/½ tsp bicarbonate of soda
   (baking soda)
175g/6oz/½ cup crunchy peanut butter
50g/2oz/generous ¼ cup caster
   (superfine) sugar
2 eggs, beaten
250ml/8fl oz/1 cup milk
25g/1oz/¼ cup roasted salted peanuts

1 Preheat the oven to 180°C/350°F/Gas 4. Grease and line a 900g/2lb loaf tin (pan) with baking parchment.

2 Sift the flour, baking powder and bicarbonate of soda together into a large bowl.

3 Put the butter and peanut butter in a large bowl and beat together with a wooden spoon to soften, then beat in the sugar until very light and fluffy.

4 Gradually whisk in the eggs a little at a time, then beat in the milk with the sifted flour and mix until incorporated.

5 Pour into the prepared tin and sprinkle the peanuts on top.

6 Bake for 1 hour, or until a skewer inserted into the centre comes out clean. Cool in the tin for 5 minutes, then turn out on to a wire rack. Remove the lining paper.

Nutritional information per portion: Energy 214kcal/904kJ; Protein 6.4g; Carbohydrate 33.5g, of which sugars 11.4g; Fat 6.9g, of which saturates 1.7g; Cholesterol 28mg; Calcium 70mg; Fibre 1.4g; Sodium 56mg.

Crunchy pear and cherry cake

This is a great cake to make with store-cupboard ingredients. With dried pears, glacé cherries and crystallized ginger, it has a lot of flavour and is finished off with a crunchy sugar topping.

SERVES 8–10

115g/4oz/1/2 cup butter, plus extra
    for greasing
115g/4oz/generous 1/2 cup caster
    (superfine) sugar
225g/8oz/2 cups plain (all-purpose) flour
10ml/2 tsp baking powder
2 eggs
60ml/4 tbsp milk
65g/21/2oz/generous 1/4 cup ready-to-
    eat dried pears, chopped
65g/21/2oz/generous 1/4 cup glacé
    (candied) cherries, washed
    and quartered
40g/11/2oz/3 tbsp chopped
    crystallized ginger
30ml/2 tbsp demerara (raw) sugar

1 Preheat the oven to 180°C/350°F/Gas 4. Grease and line a 900g/2lb loaf tin (pan) with baking parchment.

2 Put the butter and sugar in a bowl. Sift in the flour and baking powder. Add the eggs and milk, and beat for about 2 minutes, or until smooth.

3 Fold in the pears, cherries and ginger with a large metal spoon until well combined. Spoon into the tin and smooth the top level.

4 Bake for 40 minutes, then remove from the oven and quickly sprinkle the loaf with the demerara sugar.

5 Bake for a further 15–20 minutes, or until a skewer inserted into the centre comes out clean.

6 Cool in the tin for 5 minutes, then turn out on to a wire rack to go cold. Peel off the lining paper.

Nutritional information per portion: Energy 257kcal/1079kJ; Protein 4.2g; Carbohydrate 37.7g, of which sugars 20.5g; Fat 11g, of which saturates 6.6g; Cholesterol 65mg; Calcium 63mg; Fibre 1.5g; Sodium 107mg.

Parsnip, banana and orange loaf

Parsnips and bananas are full of natural sugars, which add a mellow sweetness to this cake, and the orange adds a citrus tang. Keep this cake for up to five days in an airtight container, or freeze, undecorated, for two months, tightly wrapped in foil.

SERVES 8–10

250g/9oz/2¼ cups wholemeal (whole-wheat) self-raising (self-rising) flour
15ml/1 tbsp baking powder
5ml/1 tsp ground cinnamon
5ml/1 tsp freshly ground nutmeg
130g/4½oz/7 tbsp butter
130g/4½oz/generous ½ cup soft light brown sugar
250g/9oz parsnips, peeled and coarsely grated
1 medium banana, peeled and mashed
finely grated rind and juice of 1 unwaxed orange

FOR THE TOPPING
225g/8oz cream cheese
45ml/3 tbsp icing (confectioners') sugar
juice and finely grated zest of 1 small orange

1 Preheat the oven to 180°C/350°F/ Gas 4. Grease and line a 900g/2lb loaf tin (pan) with baking parchment.

2 Sift the flour, baking powder and spices into a large bowl. Add any bran remaining in the sieve (strainer).

3 Melt the butter in a pan, add the sugar and stir until dissolved.

4 Pour the melted butter and sugar into the flour mixture. Mix in the parsnips, banana, orange rind and juice.

5 Spoon the batter into the prepared tin and level the top. Bake for 45–50 minutes until a skewer inserted into the centre of the cake comes out clean. Allow to cool before removing from the tin. Peel off the lining paper.

6 For the topping, beat together the cream cheese, icing sugar, orange juice and orange zest, until smooth. Spread evenly over the cake top.

Nutritional information per portion: Energy 246kcal/1033kJ; Protein 5.9g; Carbohydrate 35.2g, of which sugars 13.4g; Fat 10g, of which saturates 1.2g; Cholesterol 32mg; Calcium 45mg; Fibre 2.7g; Sodium 14mg.

Vanilla streusel bars

The crumbly topping on this cake makes a crunchy contrast to the moist vanilla-flavoured sponge underneath. A full flavour is achieved by using vanilla extract as well as vanilla sugar, which is easy to make at home. The bars will keep for up to four days in an airtight container.

MAKES 25 BARS

175g/6oz/³⁄₄ cup butter, softened, plus
extra for greasing
175g/6oz/1¹⁄₂ cups self-raising (self-
rising) flour
5ml/1 tsp baking powder
175g/6oz/scant 1 cup vanilla sugar
3 eggs, beaten
7.5ml/1¹⁄₂ tsp vanilla extract
15–30ml/1–2 tbsp milk

FOR THE TOPPING

115g/4oz/1 cup self-raising
(self-rising) flour
75g/3oz/6 tbsp butter
75g/3oz/6 tbsp vanilla sugar
icing (confectioners') sugar, for dusting

Nutritional information per portion: Energy 162kcal/
680kJ; Protein 2g; Carbohydrate 19.5g, of which sugars
10.7g; Fat 9g, of which saturates 5.4g; Cholesterol
44mg; Calcium 27mg; Fibre 0.4g; Sodium 70mg.

1 Preheat the oven to 180°C/350°F/ Gas 4. Lightly grease and line a 23 × 18cm/9 × 7in shallow tin (pan) with baking parchment.

2 To make the topping, sift the flour into a bowl and rub in the butter until the mixture resembles crumbs. Stir in the vanilla sugar. Set aside.

3 To make the base, sift the flour and baking powder into a bowl. Add the butter, vanilla sugar and eggs. Beat well until smooth, adding the vanilla extract and just enough milk to give a soft dropping consistency.

4 Spoon the mixture into the prepared tin and smooth level. Sprinkle the streusel topping over the surface and press down to cover the cake batter.

5 Bake for 45–60 minutes, or until browned and firm. Cool in the tin for 5 minutes.

6 Turn out on to a wire rack to go cold. Remove the lining paper.

7 Place on a board and dust with icing sugar. Cut into 25 bars with a sharp knife.

Cherry batter cake

This simple traybake is made with three contrasting layers: a cake batter, drained black cherries from a jar and a crunchy brown sugar topping. It tastes lovely with a little whipped cream. This cake can be kept for up to two days in an airtight container.

MAKES 12 SLICES

75g/3oz/6 tbsp butter, softened, plus
    extra for greasing
225g/8oz/2 cups self-raising
    (self-rising) flour
5ml/1 tsp baking powder
150g/5oz/2/3 cup soft light brown sugar
1 egg, lightly beaten
15–30ml/1–2 tbsp milk

FOR THE TOPPING

675g/11/2lb jar black cherries
175g/6oz/3/4 cup soft light brown sugar
50g/2oz/1/2 cup self-raising
    (self-rising) flour
50g/2oz/1/4 cup butter, melted
icing (confectioners') sugar, for dusting
whipped cream, to serve (optional)

1 Preheat the oven to 190°C/375°F/Gas 5. Grease a 33 x 23cm/13 x 9in Swiss roll tin (jelly roll pan). Line the base and sides with baking parchment.

2 To make the base, sift the flour and baking powder into a large bowl. Add the butter, sugar, egg and milk. Beat the mixture until smooth, then turn into the prepared tin and smooth the surface.

3 Drain the fruit and evenly distribute it over the base.

4 Mix the remaining topping ingredients together and spoon evenly over the fruit. Bake for 40 minutes, or until golden brown and firm to the touch.

5 Leave to cool in the tin. Dust with icing sugar, cut into slices, then remove from the tin.

Nutritional information per portion: Energy 314kcal/1327kJ; Protein 3.6g; Carbohydrate 57g, of which sugars 39.7g; Fat 9.5g, of which saturates 5.7g; Cholesterol 38.8mg; Calcium 74mg; Fibre 1.5g; Sodium 81mg.

Fruit malt loaf

Malt extract gives this traditional fruity loaf its wonderful chewy consistency, and wholemeal flour adds depth of flavour. Cut in slices and spread with butter, it's just right for giving to hungry children when they come home from school. Keep for up to five days in an airtight container.

SERVES 8–10

butter, for greasing
250g/9oz/2¼ cups wholemeal (whole-
    wheat) self-raising (self-rising) flour
pinch of salt
2.5ml/½ tsp bicarbonate of soda
    (baking soda)
175g/6oz/1 cup mixed dried fruit
15ml/1 tbsp malt extract
250ml/8fl oz/1 cup milk
butter, to serve

1 Preheat the oven to 160°C/325°F/Gas 3. Grease and line a 900g/2lb loaf tin (pan) with baking parchment.

2 Put the dry ingredients in a bowl.

3 Heat the malt extract and milk in a small pan, stirring until dissolved. Mix into the dry ingredients.

4 Spoon into the prepared tin. Bake for 45 minutes, or until a skewer inserted into the loaf comes out clean. Leave to stand for 5 minutes, then turn out on to a wire rack to go cold. Remove the lining paper.

Nutritional information per portion: Energy 260kcal/1103kJ; Protein 5.3g; Carbohydrate 58.6g, of which sugars 25.3g; Fat 2.1g, of which saturates 0.3g; Cholesterol 1mg; Calcium 97mg; Fibre 1.8g; Sodium 38mg.

White chocolate blondies

Blondies, like brownies, are chewy and moist squares, except that they don't usually contain chocolate. These ones, however, are made with white chocolate, sticky apricots and crunchy pecan nuts, so they are extra special. Keep for up to three days in an airtight container.

MAKES 24 SQUARES

175g/6oz/³⁄₄ cup unsalted butter, softened, plus extra for greasing

300g/11oz/generous 1¹⁄₂ cups caster (superfine) sugar

3 eggs, beaten

5ml/1 tsp vanilla extract

200g/7oz/1³⁄₄ cups plain (all-purpose) flour

5ml/1 tsp baking powder

90g/3¹⁄₂oz white chocolate chips

90g/3¹⁄₂oz/scant 1 cup pecan nuts, roughly chopped

90g/3¹⁄₂oz/scant ¹⁄₂ cup ready-to-eat dried apricots, chopped

icing (confectioners') sugar, for dusting

1 Preheat the oven to 180°C/350°F/ Gas 4. Grease and line a 30 × 20cm/ 12 × 8in shallow tin (pan) with baking parchment.

2 Beat the butter with the sugar, then add the eggs and vanilla, beating well after each addition.

3 Sift the flour and baking powder into the bowl, then add the chocolate chips, pecan nuts and apricots, and fold into the mixture until evenly blended.

4 Spoon into the prepared tin and smooth the top level.

5 Bake for 25–30 minutes, or until just set. Mark into 24 squares and leave to cool for 10 minutes.

6 Turn out on to a wire rack to go cold. Remove the lining paper, cut into squares and dust with sugar.

COOK'S TIP
Freeze, wrapped in foil, for up to 2 months.

Nutritional information per portion: Energy 183kcal/ 767kJ; Protein 1.7g; Carbohydrate 23.3g, of which sugars 16.9g; Fat 9.9g, of which saturates 4.9g; Cholesterol 17mg; Calcium 35mg; Fibre 0.7g; Sodium 60mg.

Mint choc brownies

Chocolate and mint always make a marvellous combination, but it's unusual to find them together in a cake. Here, brownies contain crisp pieces of peppermint and are covered with a minty buttercream topping. Keep for up to three days in an airtight container.

MAKES 25 SQUARES

75g/3oz/¾ cup unsweetened
   cocoa powder
175g/6oz/¾ cup soft tub margarine,
   plus extra for greasing
75g/3oz clear peppermint boiled sweets
   (hard candies)
275g/10oz/2½ cups plain
   (all-purpose) flour
7.5ml/1½ tsp bicarbonate of soda
   (baking soda)
2.5ml/½ tsp baking powder
275g/10oz/scant 1½ cups soft dark
   brown sugar
3 eggs, beaten

FOR THE TOPPING

115g/4oz/½ cup unsalted
   butter, softened
225g/8oz/2 cups icing
   (confectioners') sugar
30ml/2 tbsp milk
2.5ml/½ tsp peppermint extract
a few drops of green food colouring
thin chocolate matchsticks

1 Dissolve the cocoa powder in 350ml/12fl oz/1½ cups boiling water, stir, then leave for 30 minutes.

2 Preheat the oven to 180°C/350°F/ Gas 4. Grease and line a 23cm/9in square deep cake tin (pan) with baking parchment.

3 Put the boiled mints into a strong plastic bag and tap with a rolling pin until they break into small pieces.

4 Sift the flour, bicarbonate of soda and baking powder into the cocoa.

5 Add the margarine, sugar and eggs. Beat for 2 minutes.

6 Fold in the crushed mints. Spoon into the tin. Smooth the top level.

7 Bake for 70 minutes, cool in the tin.

8 To make the topping, beat the butter with the icing sugar, milk, peppermint extract and a few drops of green food colouring. Spread over the cooled cake.

9 Cut into squares and decorate each with two small matchsticks.

Nutritional information per portion: Energy 331kcal/ 1379kJ; Protein 3.8g; Carbohydrate 30.2g, of which sugars 21.4g; Fat 22.5g, of which saturates 6.7g; Cholesterol 49mg; Calcium 37mg; Fibre 1.1g; Sodium 50mg.

Florentine slices

If you're looking for a popular cake for a cake sale or coffee morning, you'll find the colourful jewel-like topping on these fruity slices makes them a great seller – and they'll also be snapped up at home in no time. These cakes keep in an airtight container for up to four days.

MAKES 12 SLICES

150g/5oz/10 tbsp butter, plus extra
    for greasing
150g/5oz/²⁄₃ cup golden caster
    (superfine) sugar
3 eggs
175g/6oz/1¹⁄₂ cups self-raising (self-
    rising) flour
275g/10oz/1²⁄₃ cups mixed dried fruit

90g/3¹⁄₂oz/generous ¹⁄₂ cup glacé
    (candied) cherries, halved
a few drops of almond extract

FOR THE TOPPING
100g/4oz/¹⁄₂ cup glacé (candied)
    cherries, chopped
15ml/1 tbsp golden (light corn) syrup
50g/2oz/¹⁄₂ cup flaked (sliced) almonds
25g/1oz/2 tbsp angelica, chopped

1 Preheat the oven to 190°C/375°F/ Gas 5. Grease and line a 28 × 18cm/11 × 7in shallow cake tin (pan) with baking parchment.

2 Whisk the butter and sugar until light and fluffy. Whisk in the eggs one at a time and fold in the flour. Set aside 30ml/2 tbsp of the mixture.

3 Fold the dried fruit, cherries and almond extract into the remaining cake mixture, then spoon into the tin and smooth the top level.

4 Bake for 20 minutes, reduce the heat to 180°C/350°F/Gas 4. Bake for a further 15 minutes, until just set.

5 To make the topping, stir the chopped cherries into the reserved cake mixture with the syrup, almonds and angelica, and mix well.

6 Spread evenly over the cake top using a wetted spoon. Bake for 15 minutes. Leave to cool in the tin.

7 Loosen the lining papers. Cut into 12 fingers when cold.

Nutritional information per portion: Energy 340kcal/ 1429kJ; Protein 4.6g; Carbohydrate 51.7g, of which sugars 40.8g; Fat 14.2g, of which saturates 7.4g; Cholesterol 76mg; Calcium 101mg; Fibre 1.4g; Sodium 177mg.

Sticky toffee traybake

Dates add moisture and richness to cake mixtures, and make this traybake particularly gooey. With their luscious toffee layer these cake squares are wickedly delicious. They are perfect for toffee fans everywhere. The cakes keep for up to three days in an airtight container.

MAKES 15 SQUARES

50g/2oz/¼ cup butter, diced, plus extra
   for greasing
150g/5oz/scant 1 cup chopped stoned
   (pitted) dates
5ml/1 tsp bicarbonate of soda
   (baking soda)
150g/5oz/1¼ cups plain
   (all-purpose) flour
5ml/1 tsp baking powder
200g/7oz/1 cup caster (superfine) sugar
50g/2oz/½ cup walnuts, chopped
1 large (US extra large) egg, beaten
2.5ml/½ tsp vanilla extract

FOR THE ICING

25g/1oz/2 tbsp unsalted butter
60ml/4 tbsp soft light brown sugar
60ml/4 tbsp double (heavy) cream

1 Preheat the oven to 180°C/350°F/ Gas 4. Grease and line a 30 × 20cm/12 × 8in shallow baking tin (pan) with baking parchment.

2 Put the dates in a bowl with the bicarbonate of soda and pour over 250ml/8fl oz/1 cup boiling water. Stir, then leave to cool slightly while making the batter.

3 Sift the flour and baking powder into a bowl and add the butter. Rub between your fingertips until the mixture resembles fine crumbs.

4 Stir in the sugar and walnuts, and mix well. Add the egg and vanilla extract with the date mixture and beat until smooth.

5 Spoon into the baking tin and smooth the top level. Bake for 25–30 minutes, or until well risen and firm to the touch. Leave to cool in the tin for 5 minutes, then turn out to cool on a wire rack and peel away the lining paper.

6 Put the icing ingredients in a pan and stir over a low heat until the sugar dissolves. Bring to the boil and boil for 1–2 minutes, until thickened.

7 Pour over the cake. Leave to set. Cut into 15 squares.

Nutritional information per portion: Energy 565kcal/ 2356kJ; Protein 6.2g; Carbohydrate 52.8g, of which sugars 38.8g; Fat 38.1g, of which saturates 20.7g; Cholesterol 175mg; Calcium 130mg; Fibre 0.8g; Sodium 349mg.

Little Cakes

Miniature cakes such as cupcakes, whoopie pies and cake pops are fun to make and eat. This section contains a fantastic variety of fanciful mini cakes – choose from Spangled Sugar Cupcakes, with a lovely sugar decoration, towering Montebianco cupcakes or Cupcakes with Raspberry Buttercream. Make any party go with a swing with Banoffee and Walnut Whoopie Pies, Red Velvet Pops or Birthday Cake Pops.

Fondant fancies

A classic fondant coating is light and shiny, and ideal to finish these delicate little cakes. The fancies are extra special, so serve them for a classic celebration such as a christening. They will keep for two days in an airtight container. Freeze the undecorated base for up to three months.

MAKES 28

50g/2oz/¹/₂ cup unsalted butter
 oil, for greasing
3 large (US extra large) eggs
100g/3³/₄oz/generous ¹/₂ cup caster
 (superfine) sugar
100g/3³/₄oz/scant 1 cup plain (all-
 purpose) flour
15ml/1 tbsp cornflour (cornstarch)
pinch of salt

**FOR THE ICING AND
DECORATION**
500g/1lb/5 cups fondant icing
 sugar, sifted
food colourings

1 Melt the butter in a small pan over a gentle heat and allow to cool.

2 Preheat the oven to 180°C/350°F/ Gas 4. Oil and line a 28 × 18cm/ 11 × 7in baking tin with baking parchment.

3 In a large bowl, whisk the eggs and sugar together, using an electric mixer, until pale, thick and creamy, and the mixture leaves a trail when the beaters are lifted away.

4 Sift the flour, cornflour and salt over the surface.

5 Pour the melted butter around the sides of the bowl. Gently fold together, taking care not to knock out the air, then pour into the lined tin.

6 Bake for 20 minutes, or until light golden and just firm to the touch.

7 Cool in the tin for 5 minutes, then turn out, peel away the lining paper and leave on a wire rack until cold.

8 Stamp out rounds using a 3.5cm/ 1¹/₂in pastry (cookie) cutter, fancy shapes or small squares, and put on a wire rack standing over a tray.

9 Put the sifted fondant icing sugar into a bowl and add enough cold water to give a coating consistency. Divide the icing among several bowls and colour it delicately with a few drops of food colouring. Keep each bowl covered with a damp cloth until needed.

10 Working quickly, spoon the icing over each cake and smooth down to cover the tops and sides. Put in paper cases to serve.

Nutritional information per portion: Energy 259kcal/ 1094kJ; Protein 2.7g; Carbohydrate 49.7g, of which sugars 41.4g; Fat 6.9g, of which saturates 4g; Cholesterol 40mg; Calcium 50mg; Fibre 0.3g; Sodium 66mg.

Marshmallow daisy cakes

These lemony cakes are as fresh as a daisy; they are quick and very simple to make and bake. The marshmallow flowers take moments to create – all you need is a pair of scissors. They are sure to be a hit, especially with children, and will keep for two days in an airtight container.

MAKES 12

115g/4oz/1 cup self-raising
   (self-rising) flour
5ml/1 tsp baking powder
115g/4oz/generous 1/2 cup caster
   (superfine) sugar
115g/4oz/1/2 cup soft tub margarine
2 large (US extra large) eggs, beaten
15ml/1 tbsp lemon juice
finely grated rind of 1 lemon

FOR THE DECORATION
1/2 quantity buttercream, see page 218
12 pink and white marshmallows
caster (superfine) sugar, for dusting
small sweets (candies)

1 Preheat the oven to 180°C/350°F/ Gas 4. Line a 12-cup muffin tin (pan) with paper cases.

2 Sift the flour, baking powder and sugar into a large bowl, then add the remaining ingredients. Beat until light and creamy, then place heaped spoonfuls into the paper cases.

3 Bake for about 20 minutes, or until golden and firm to the touch.

4 Allow to cool for 2 minutes, then turn out on to a wire rack to go cold.

5 When cold, spread the top of each cake with a little buttercream.

6 Use kitchen scissors to cut each marshmallow in half horizontally.

7 Dip the cut marshmallow edges in sugar to prevent sticking. Repeat, cutting the marshmallows in half again, dipping the cut edge in sugar.

8 Press the tips of four halves together to form four petals of a flower. Arrange them on top of a cupcake and press a small sweet into the centre.

Nutritional information per portion: Energy 115kcal/ 483kJ; Protein 1.3g; Carbohydrate 16.5g, of which sugars 12.1g; Fat 5.4g, of which saturates 3.2g; Cholesterol 31mg; Calcium 18mg; Fibre 0.2g; Sodium 43mg.

Snowballs

These snowy muffins prove that variations on this simple theme appear to be endless. They have a tasty topping, white chocolate with coconut liqueur and cream, sprinkled with coconut strands.

MAKES 12

175g/6oz/12 tbsp caster
  (superfine) sugar
2.5ml/¹/₂ tsp baking powder
200g/7oz/1³/₄ cups self-raising
  (self-rising) flour
15ml/2 tbsp desiccated (dry
  unsweetened shredded) coconut
175g/6oz/³/₄ cup soft tub margarine
3 eggs, beaten
15ml/1 tbsp milk

FOR THE TOPPING

175g/6oz white chocolate, chopped
15ml/1 tbsp coconut liqueur
75ml/5 tbsp double (heavy) cream
175g/6oz/2 cups large shredded coconut
  strands or curls

1 Preheat the oven to 180°C/350°F/Gas 4. Line a 12-cup deep muffin tin (pan) with paper cases.

2 Sift the sugar, baking powder, flour and coconut into a large bowl. Add the margarine, eggs and milk and beat until smooth and creamy. Divide the batter evenly among the paper cases.

3 Bake for 18–20 minutes, or until risen, golden and firm to the touch. Leave in the tin for 2 minutes, then transfer to a wire rack to cool.

4 To make the topping, put the chocolate and liqueur in a bowl. Put the cream in a pan and bring to the boil, then pour it over the chocolate and liqueur. Stir until smooth, then cool and chill for 30 minutes. Whisk with an electric mixer for a few minutes, or until light and fluffy.

5 Spread the icing over the top of each muffin, then sprinkle coconut strands liberally over the icing to cover completely.

Nutritional information per portion: Energy 481kcal/2005kJ; Protein 5.9g; Carbohydrate 39.6g, of which sugars 35.2g; Fat 34.3g, of which saturates 23.9g; Cholesterol 12mg; Calcium 137mg; Fibre 3g; Sodium 167mg.

Rich chocolate ruffles

These glossy chocolate cakes are a class act, decorated with ruffles of chocolate and glinting with gold leaf. Each one is in a gold foil case to make them perfect for a special occasion.

MAKES 12

65g/2¹/₂oz/9 tbsp self-raising (self-rising) flour
25g/1oz/¹/₄ cup unsweetened cocoa powder
75g/3oz/¹/₃ cup soft dark brown sugar
75g/3oz/6 tbsp butter, softened
3 eggs
30ml/2 tbsp milk

FOR THE RUFFLES

125g/4oz plain (semisweet) chocolate, grated
37.5ml/2¹/₂ tbsp liquid glucose (clear corn syrup)

FOR THE TOPPING

100ml/3¹/₂fl oz/scant ¹/₂ cup double (heavy) cream
15ml/1 tbsp liquid glucose (clear corn syrup)
200g/7oz dark (bittersweet) chocolate, melted
scraps of edible gold leaf (optional)

1 Preheat the oven to 190°C/375°F/Gas 5. Line a 12-cup muffin tray with gold foil cases.

2 Sift the flour and cocoa into a bowl, add the sugar, butter, eggs and milk, and beat for about 2 minutes, or until smooth. Divide the batter among the cases and bake for 15 minutes, or until just firm to the touch in the centre. Remove from the tray and leave to cool on a wire rack.

3 To make the ruffles, melt the chocolate in a heatproof bowl set over a pan of warm water. Remove from the heat. Beat in the glucose until a paste forms that comes away from the sides. Chill in a plastic bag for 1 hour. Break off pieces and knead until pliable. Roll out between sheets of non-stick paper until 5mm/¹/₄in thick. Mould into delicate fans.

4 To make the topping, bring the cream to the boil in a pan. Remove from the heat, add the liquid glucose and the melted chocolate, and stir.

5 Spoon the mixture over the top of each cake, top with a chocolate ruffle and tiny scraps of gold leaf, if you like, then leave to set. Eat fresh for the best taste.

Nutritional information per portion: Energy 392kcal/1641kJ; Protein 5g; Carbohydrate 42.2g, of which sugars 30.5g; Fat 23.8g, of which saturates 14.8g; Cholesterol 111mg; Calcium 110mg; Fibre 0.7g; Sodium 235mg.

Spangled sugar cupcakes

These cakes are made using a basic mixture, but are transformed by the original decoration using caramelized sugar spirals, which are not difficult to make.

MAKES 8–9

175g/6oz/¾ cup butter, softened

175g/6oz/¾ cup caster (superfine) sugar

5ml/1 tsp finely grated lemon rind

4 eggs, lightly beaten

175g/6oz/1½ cups self-raising
   (self-rising) flour, sifted

115g/4oz cinder toffee (honeycomb), broken
   into small pieces

**FOR THE PULLED SUGAR
DECORATIONS**

115g/4oz/½ cup caster
   (superfine) sugar

1 Preheat the oven to 180°C/350°F/Gas 4. Line the cups of a bun tin (pan) with paper cake cases. Beat the butter with the sugar until light and creamy. Add the lemon rind. Gradually add the eggs in small amounts, beating after each addition.

2 Add the sifted flour and fold lightly into the mixture until just combined. Fold in the cinder toffee.

3 Spoon the mixture into the paper cases and bake for 20 minutes until the cakes are golden and firm. Allow to cool a little in the tin, then turn out on to a rack to cool completely.

4 To make the decorations, place the caster sugar in a non-stick pan over a high heat. Do not stir. When the sugar starts to turn into syrup around the edges tilt the pan to blend the sugar into the syrup. Continue until all the sugar has melted into a golden caramel. Remove the pan immediately from the heat and briefly sink its base in cold water. As the caramel cools it will become thicker; for sugar spirals it needs to be the consistency of golden (corn) syrup. If it thickens too much, gently warm it up.

5 To make the spirals, take one tablespoonful of the caramel and trail it over a greased sharpening steel, while turning the steel. Snap off the tail of the caramel and gently slide the spiral off. Leave on a lightly oiled tray while you make the remaining decorations. Gently press the sugar spirals at an angle on top of the cakes. Serve in cups, if you like.

Nutritional information per portion: Energy 569kcal/2379kJ; Protein 5.6g; Carbohydrate 61.6g, of which sugars 46.7g; Fat 37.7g, of which saturates 21.7g; Cholesterol 173mg; Calcium 81mg; Fibre 0.6g; Sodium 203mg.

Pistachio flower cakes

The pistachios add flavour and a delicate green colour to a basic friand cake mixture, which is lightly perfumed with rose water. These cakes will delight lovers of Parisian-style confections.

MAKES 12

175g/6oz/³⁄₄ cup butter, melted
5ml/1 tsp rose water
150g/5oz/1¹⁄₄ cups finely ground
   pistachios, sifted
225g/8oz/2 cups icing (confectioners')
   sugar, sifted, plus extra for dusting

70g/2¹⁄₂ oz/9 tbsp plain (all-purpose)
   flour, sifted
6 egg whites
2.5ml/¹⁄₂ tsp finely grated lemon rind
whole pistachio nuts, to
   decorate (optional)

1 Preheat the oven to 190°C/375°F/Gas 5. Grease 12 fluted bun tins (pans) with melted butter and dust lightly with flour.

2 Mix the melted butter and rose water in a small bowl, then set aside.

3 Put the ground pistachios in a large mixing bowl, reserving 25g/1oz for decorating the cakes. Stir in the sifted icing sugar and flour.

4 In a separate bowl, beat the egg whites lightly just to break them up. Add the egg whites to the dry ingredients and mix. Add the melted butter and lemon rind to the bowl and mix until just combined.

5 Pour the mixture into the prepared tins and bake for 16 minutes, until golden and springy. Leave to cool slightly then turn out on to a wire rack to go cold.

6 Dust with the reserved ground pistachios. Half-cover them with a strip of paper and dust with icing sugar, then remove the paper and decorate with a few pistachio nuts.

Nutritional information per portion: Energy 282kcal/1177kJ; Protein 4.4g; Carbohydrate 25.2g, of which sugars 20.4g; Fat 18.9g, of which saturates 8.8g; Cholesterol 34mg; Calcium 35mg; Fibre 0.9g; Sodium 207mg.

Pistachio and rose water cupcakes

Rose water and pistachios have a subtle affinity, and are used in this recipe to flavour a rich buttercream frosting. The green colour of the topping gives them an unusual appearance.

MAKES 8–9

175g/6oz/³⁄₄ cup butter, softened
175g/6oz/³⁄₄ cup caster (superfine) sugar
5ml/1 tsp vanilla extract
4 eggs, lightly beaten
175g/6oz/1¹⁄₂ cups self-raising
    (self-rising) flour, sifted

FOR THE TOPPING

115g/4oz/³⁄₄ cup pistachio nuts, shelled
140g/5oz/10 tbsp butter
115g/4oz/1 cup icing (confectioners')
    sugar, sifted
10ml/2 tsp milk
2–3 drops rose water, or to taste

1 Preheat the oven to 180°C/ 350°F/Gas 4. Line 8–9 cups of a bun tin (pan) with paper cases. Beat together the butter and sugar until light and creamy. Add the vanilla.

2 Gradually add the eggs, beating well after each addition. Add the flour and fold it into the mixture.

3 Divide the mixture among the paper cases and bake for 20 minutes until the cakes are golden and firm to the touch.

4 Leave to cool for 5 minutes, then turn the cakes out on to a wire rack to cool before decorating.

5 For the topping, process the pistachio nuts in a blender until finely ground. Whisk the butter until soft and creamy. Whisking at a low speed, gradually beat in the sugar, pistachios and milk, alternating with the rose water, until smooth.

6 Cover the cakes with the frosting and sprinkle a few chopped pistachios over the top of each.

COOK'S TIP

Because of their oil content, store pistachios in the freezer rather than at room temperature. Pack them in airtight containers or sealed freezer bags.

Nutritional information per portion: Energy 566kcal/ 2357kJ; Protein 8.5g; Carbohydrate 47.5g, of which sugars 32.2g; Fat 39.4g, of which saturates 19.2g; Cholesterol 157mg; Calcium 84mg; Fibre 1.8g; Sodium 375mg.

Montebianco cupcakes

This recipe is based on a pudding called Marrons Mont Blanc in France and Montebianco in Italy: a sweetened chestnut purée covered in thick vanilla cream. Anyone with a sweet tooth and a love of chestnuts will find these little cakes especially delicious.

MAKES 10

75g/3oz/6 tbsp butter, softened
175g/6oz/3/4 cup golden caster (superfine) sugar
115g/4oz/1 cup icing (confectioners') sugar
5ml/1 tsp vanilla extract
15ml/1 tbsp rum
4 eggs, separated
200g/7oz cooked and peeled whole chestnuts, ground

150g/5oz/11/4 cups plain (all-purpose) flour
10ml/2 tsp baking powder

FOR THE TOPPING
300ml/1/2 pint/11/4 cups double (heavy) cream
5ml/1 tsp vanilla extract
10ml/2 tsp caster (superfine) sugar
sifted cocoa powder, to dust

1 Preheat the oven to 180°C/350°F/Gas 4. Line the cups of a bun tin (pan) with paper cases.

2 Place the butter, caster sugar and icing sugar in a large bowl and beat until light and smooth using an electric mixer. Mix in the vanilla extract and rum. Beat the egg yolks lightly and add them in a thin stream, beating well until the mixture is very smooth. Add the ground chestnuts and beat them in, then fold in the flour sifted together with the baking powder.

3 In a separate bowl beat the egg whites into fairly firm peaks and fold them lightly into the chestnut mixture until evenly combined.

4 Fill the cups three-quarters full with the cake mixture, and bake for 20–25 minutes, until the cakes are golden and the centres feel springy. Remove from the oven.

5 Leave the cakes in the tins for 5 minutes to cool, then turn them out on to a wire rack to cool.

6 To make the topping, beat the cream with the vanilla extract and caster sugar into soft peaks that hold their shape. Transfer to a large piping (pastry) bag fitted with a plain 5mm/1/4in nozzle and pipe into tall piles on top of the cakes. To finish, dust the cream lightly with sifted cocoa powder.

Nutritional information per portion: Energy 429kcal/1796kJ; Protein 5g; Carbohydrate 51.1g, of which sugars 33.8g; Fat 25.2g, of which saturates 13.8g; Cholesterol 132mg; Calcium 74mg; Fibre 1.3g; Sodium 100mg.

Madeleine cakes with raspberry buttercream

These madeleine-style cupcakes have a gorgeous pink crumb and little shell-shaped decorations made from the same mixture, pressed over a glamorous pink swirl of raspberry buttercream.

MAKES 9

115g/4oz/½ cup butter, melted
115g/4oz/1 cup self-raising
   (self-rising) flour
salt
100g/3½ oz/scant ½ cup caster
   (superfine) sugar
3 eggs
50g/2oz/½ cup ground almonds
5ml/1 tsp rose water

FOR THE TOPPING

75g/3oz/6 tbsp butter, softened
175g/6oz/1½ cups icing (confectioners')
   sugar, sifted
15ml/1 tbsp lemon juice
15ml/1 tbsp raspberry jam
few drops red food colouring

1 Preheat the oven to 190°C/375°F/ Gas 5. Line 9 cups of a muffin tin (pan) with paper cases. Brush 9 mini madeleine moulds with melted butter.

2 Sift the flour and salt into a bowl and stir in the sugar. Beat the eggs and mix into the sugar and flour, then add the cooled melted butter, ground almonds and rose water. Mix well. Cover and chill for 1 hour.

3 Fill the paper cases three-quarters full. Half-fill the mini madeleine mould with mixture. Bake the cupcakes for 5 minutes.

4 Bake the cakes for 20 minutes until risen and firm. Leave to cool then transfer to a wire rack.

5 For the topping, beat the butter with the icing sugar until smooth. Stir in the lemon juice and jam and beat. Add a few drops of food colouring and beat until evenly coloured.

6 Fill a piping (pastry) bag fitted with a star nozzle with the buttercream. Pipe a whirl over the centre of each cake and press a madeleine lightly to one side of it.

Nutritional information per portion: Energy 364kcal/ 1523kJ; Protein 4.7g; Carbohydrate 39.3g, of which sugars 29.4g; Fat 22.1g, of which saturates 12g; Cholesterol 111mg; Calcium 58mg; Fibre 0.8g; Sodium 182mg.

Fresh fruit-topped cupcakes

Use summer fruits and a dusting of icing sugar to dress up basic cupcakes. This luxurious way to serve them means they'll go down well with adults as well as children.

MAKES 8–9

175g/6oz/¾ cup butter, softened
175g/6oz/¾ cup caster (superfine) sugar
5ml/1 tsp vanilla extract, or 5ml/
   1 tsp finely grated lemon rind
4 eggs, lightly beaten
175g/6oz/1½ cups self-raising
   (self-rising) flour, sifted

FOR THE TOPPING

400ml/14fl oz/1⅔ cups whipping cream
275g/10 oz mixed berries
icing (confectioners') sugar, for dusting

1 Preheat the oven to 180°C/350°F/ Gas 4. Line 8–9 cups of a bun tin (pan) with paper cases. Place the butter and sugar in a large mixing bowl.

2 Beat together until light and creamy. Add the vanilla or lemon rind. Gradually add the eggs, beating after each addition. Add the flour and fold into the mixture until just combined.

3 Divide the mixture among the paper cases and bake for 20 minutes until golden brown and the centres feel firm to the touch.

4 Remove from the oven. Leave to cool for 5 minutes, then transfer the cakes to a wire rack to cool completely before decorating.

5 Scoop out a circle of sponge from the top of the cakes using a small sharp knife. Set the lids to one side. Whip the cream until stiff peaks form. Place a spoonful of cream in each sponge and top with fruit. Replace the lids at an angle and dust with icing sugar.

COOK'S TIP

To make ahead, store cupcakes in an airtight container, or, freeze undecorated. Use new paper cases for serving them.

Nutritional information per portion: Energy 536kcal/ 2253kJ; Protein 5.6g; Carbohydrate 78.4g, of which sugars 74.9g; Fat 24.4g, of which saturates 11.4g; Cholesterol 107mg; Calcium 87mg; Fibre 1.1g; Sodium 171mg.

Cupcakes with raspberry buttercream

This mouthwatering raspberry pink cream is great for party cakes, when it is piped into little rosettes. Top these cakes with a few fresh raspberries for an elegant finish.

MAKES 8–9

175g/6oz/¾ cup butter, softened
175g/6oz/¾ cup caster (superfine) sugar
5ml/1 tsp vanilla extract, or 5ml/
   1 tsp finely grated lemon rind
4 eggs, lightly beaten
175g/6oz/1½ cups self-raising (self-rising)
   flour, sifted

FOR THE TOPPING

175g/6oz/¾ cup butter, softened
350g/12oz/3 cups icing (confectioners')
   sugar, sifted
25ml/1½ tbsp lemon juice
25ml/1½ tbsp raspberry jam
few drops red food colouring
fresh raspberries

1 Preheat the oven to 180°C/350°F/Gas 4. Line 8–9 cups of a bun tin (pan) with paper cases.

2 Beat the butter and sugar together until light and creamy. Add the vanilla or lemon rind.

3 Gradually add the eggs, beating well after each addition. Add the sifted flour and fold into the mixture until just combined.

4 Divide the mixture among the paper cases and bake for 20 minutes until the cakes are golden brown and the centres feel firm to the touch. Remove from the oven.

5 Leave to cool in the tin for 5 minutes, then transfer to a wire rack to cool completely.

6 For the topping, beat the butter with the icing sugar until smooth and fluffy. Stir in the lemon juice and raspberry jam and continue to beat until smooth. Add the food colouring and beat until the buttercream is evenly coloured a pale pink.

7 Fill a piping (pastry) bag fitted with a star nozzle with the buttercream, and pipe small shell shapes on to the cooled cakes. Decorate with fresh raspberries.

Nutritional information per portion: Energy 618kcal/2587kJ; Protein 5g; Carbohydrate 76.8g, of which sugars 62.4g; Fat 34.5g, of which saturates 21.7g; Cholesterol 174mg; Calcium 118mg; Fibre 0.6g; Sodium 396mg.

Iced cherry cakes

Glacé cherries are used in this almond cake mixture, but you could use sharp-tasting dried sour cherries, or even fresh cherries. A textured rolling pin is used for the embossed basketweave icing.

MAKES 10

175g/6oz/1½ cups self-raising (self-rising) flour
10ml/2 tsp baking powder
75g/3oz/¾ cup ground almonds
175g/6oz/¾ cup butter, softened
175g/6oz/¾ cup golden caster (superfine) sugar
3 eggs, lightly beaten
finely grated rind of ½ lemon
finely grated rind of ½ orange
15ml/1 tbsp brandy or Calvados

60ml/4 tbsp orange juice
150g/5oz glacé (candied) cherries, halved

FOR THE TOPPING
350g/12oz sugarpaste
green food colouring

FOR THE DECORATIONS
150g/5oz sugarpaste
red and brown food colouring
115g/4oz royal icing

1 Preheat the oven to 180°C/350°F/Gas 4. Line the cups of a bun tin (pan) with paper cases.

2 Sift the flour and baking powder into a large mixing bowl and stir in the ground almonds.

3 In another bowl beat the butter and sugar until creamy. Add one egg at a time and beat until the mixture is light and fluffy. Mix in the fruit rind, brandy and orange juice, then the dry ingredients and the cherries.

4 Fill the paper cases three-quarters full. Bake for 25 minutes or until golden and springy to the touch. Leave to cool a little before turning them out on to a wire rack.

5 For the topping, colour the sugarpaste pale green and roll it out to a 6mm/¼in thickness. Emboss with a decorative rolling pin, then cut out 10 circles and stick them on the cooled cakes using royal icing. Roll 20 red sugarpaste cherries, 20 brown stems and some green leaves and stick in place.

Nutritional information per portion: Energy 548kcal/2308kJ; Protein 5.6g; Carbohydrate 90.4g, of which sugars 76.9g; Fat 20.4g, of which saturates 10.3g; Cholesterol 97mg; Calcium 96mg; Fibre 1.2g; Sodium 162mg.

Strawberry cakes

This pretty decorative design has to be assembled just before serving so that the fresh fruit doesn't discolour the sugarpaste topping. All the components can be made ahead of time though.

MAKES 10

2 eggs
115g/4oz/$\frac{1}{2}$ cup caster (superfine) sugar
50ml/2fl oz/$\frac{1}{4}$ cup double
   (heavy) cream
finely grated rind of 1 lemon
115g/4oz/1 cup self-raising
   (self-rising) flour
2.5ml/$\frac{1}{2}$ tsp baking powder
50g/2oz/4 tbsp butter, melted

FOR THE DECORATION
strawberry jam
small quantity sugarpaste
pink and green food colouring
2 sizes of sugarpaste strawberry flowers
icing (confectioners') sugar, for dusting
fresh strawberries

1 Preheat the oven to 180°C/ 350°F/Gas 4 and line 10 holes of a bun tin (pan) with paper cases. Beat the eggs with the sugar. Beat in the cream for 1 minute, then add the lemon rind. Sift the flour with the baking powder, then fold lightly into the mixture, followed by the butter.

2 Three-quarters fill the paper cases. Bake for 15 minutes until risen and golden. Allow to cool in the tin for 5 minutes, then turn out on to a wire rack to cool.

3 Coat the top of each cake with strawberry jam. Tint some sugarpaste pink and roll out thinly on a surface dusted with icing sugar. Stamp out circles to fit the top of the cupcakes. Stick in place on top of the jam.

4 Tint another small amount of sugarpaste green. Roll out and cut out leaves and calyx shapes. Using glacé icing, stick in place.

5 Stick a leaf on one side of the cupcake top. Decide where the strawberry will go and position the strawberry flowers close by. Wrap the calyx over the top of the strawberry. Use jam to hold it in place and stick on top of the cake just before serving.

Nutritional information per portion: Energy 243kcal/ 1024kJ; Protein 2.6g; Carbohydrate 43.4g, of which sugars 34.6g; Fat 8g, of which saturates 4.5g; Cholesterol 56mg, Calcium 42mg, Fibre 0.4g, Sodium 56mg.

Pear cakes with curled marzipan leaves

The glorious shapes and colours of fallen leaves inspired the decoration for these delicious cakes made with caramelized autumn fruit. If you prefer to make standard-sized cupcakes, cut the pears into chunks instead of halves.

MAKES 6–7 LARGE CAKES

3–4 small ripe pears
40g/1½ oz/3 tbsp butter
15ml/1 tbsp caster (superfine) sugar
45ml/3 tbsp water
225g/8oz/2 cups plain (all-purpose) flour
15ml/1 tbsp baking powder
10ml/2 tsp mixed (apple pie) spice
150g/5oz/¾ cup golden caster
  (superfine) sugar

1 egg, lightly beaten
5ml/1 tsp finely grated lemon rind
75g/3oz/6 tbsp butter, melted
300ml/½ pint/1¼ cups sour cream
20 pecan nuts, lightly crushed
50g/2oz marzipan
orange food colouring
sifted icing (confectioners') sugar

1 Preheat the oven to 180°C/350°F/Gas 4. Grease 6–7 10cm/4in-diameter muffin tins (pans) or line with mini panettone paper cases.

2 Peel and cut the pears into halves lengthways. Remove the cores but leave the short stems on the fruit if possible.

3 Place the butter, sugar and water in a small frying pan over a low to medium heat, then sauté the pear halves gently for 6 minutes until tender. Set aside to cool.

4 Sift the dry ingredients into a large bowl. In another bowl, stir the egg, lemon rind, warm melted butter and sour cream together, then gently fold into the dry ingredients, with the pecans, until blended.

5 Add a small amount of batter to each cup. Press one pear half into each, upright, then half-fill the tins with the remaining batter. Bake for 25 minutes. Leave to cool for 5 minutes, then turn out on to a rack.

6 Colour the marzipan, then roll out thinly. Cut out leaves with a cutter. Drape over a rolling pin to dry. Paint veins on the leaves with food colouring. Serve the cakes dusted with icing sugar and decorated with the leaves.

Nutritional information per portion: Energy 566kcal/2362kJ; Protein 7.1g; Carbohydrate 58.7g, of which sugars 33.9g; Fat 35.2g, of which saturates 15.5g; Cholesterol 91mg; Calcium 121mg; Fibre 3.2g; Sodium 155mg.

Chocolate mint-filled cupcakes

These dark chocolate cakes have a sensational surprise inside: a luscious mint cream filling. For even more mint flavour, try folding eight chopped mint chocolates into the cake batter.

MAKES 12

150g/5oz/²/₃ cup unsalted (sweet)
    butter, softened
300g/11oz/1½ cups caster
    (superfine) sugar
3 eggs
250ml/8fl oz/1 cup milk
5ml/1 tsp peppermint extract
225g/8oz/2 cups plain (all-purpose) flour
pinch of salt
5ml/1 tsp bicarbonate of soda (baking soda)
50g/2oz/½ cup unsweetened
    cocoa powder

FOR THE FILLING AND TOPPING

300ml/10fl oz/1¼ cups whipping cream
10ml/2 tsp peppermint extract
175g/6oz plain (semisweet) chocolate
115g/4oz/½ cup butter

1 Preheat the oven to 180°C/350°F/Gas 4. Arrange 12 paper cases in a bun tin (pan).

2 Beat together the butter and sugar until creamy. Beat in the eggs, milk and peppermint. Sift the flour, salt, bicarbonate of soda and cocoa powder over the batter and mix in. Fill the cases with the batter. Bake for 15 minutes, until a skewer inserted into the centre comes out clean. Cool on a wire rack.

3 For the filling, whip the cream with 5ml/1tsp of the peppermint until it holds its shape. Pipe about 15ml/1 tbsp into the centre of each muffin.

4 To make the topping, in a pan over a low heat melt the chocolate and butter. Remove from the heat and stir in the remaining peppermint extract.

5 Leave to cool, then spread on to the top of each of the cupcakes.

Nutritional information per portion: Energy 555kcal/2315kJ; Protein 6.1g; Carbohydrate 52.3g, of which sugars 36.8g; Fat 38.6g, of which saturates 23.1g; Cholesterol 133mg; Calcium 98mg; Fibre 1.1g; Sodium 247mg.

Blueberry and chocolate cupcakes

Blueberries are one of the many fruits that combine deliciously with the richness of chocolate in cakes, while still retaining their own distinctive flavour.

MAKES 12

115g/4oz/½ cup butter
75g/3oz plain (semisweet)
    chocolate, chopped
200g/7oz/scant 1 cup sugar
1 egg, lightly beaten
250ml/8fl oz/1 cup buttermilk
10ml/2 tsp vanilla extract
275g/10oz/2½ cups plain
    (all-purpose) flour
5ml/1 tsp bicarbonate of soda
    (baking soda)
175g/6oz/generous 1 cup fresh or
    thawed frozen blueberries
25g/1oz plain (semisweet) chocolate,
    melted, to decorate

1 Preheat the oven to 190°C/375°F/Gas 5. Arrange 12 paper cases in a muffin tin (pan). Melt the butter and chocolate in a pan over a medium heat, stirring frequently, until smooth. Remove from the heat and allow to cool slightly.

2 Put the sugar in a mixing bowl, add the egg, buttermilk and vanilla extract, and pour in the chocolate mixture. Stir until smooth. Sift the flour and bicarbonate of soda over the mixture, then gently fold in until just blended. (The mixture should be slightly lumpy.)

3 Gently fold in the blueberries. Spoon the batter into the paper cases. Bake for 25–30 minutes, until a skewer inserted in the centre comes out with just a few crumbs attached. Remove from the oven and leave in the tin for 5 minutes, then transfer the muffins to a wire rack to cool.

4 If serving warm, drizzle melted chocolate over the top of each, then serve. Otherwise, leave until cold before decorating.

Nutritional information per portion: Energy 203kcal/850kJ; Protein 3.9g; Carbohydrate 24.9g, of which sugars 6.6g; Fat 10.5g, of which saturates 6.4g; Cholesterol 39mg; Calcium 63mg; Fibre 1g; Sodium 90mg.

Chocolate fairy cakes

These magical little treats are sure to enchant adults and children alike. The chocolate sponge is rich, moist and dark, and contrasts appetizingly with the pure white vanilla-flavoured buttercream.

MAKES 24

175g/6oz/³⁄₄ cup butter, softened
150ml/¹⁄₄ pint/²⁄₃ cup milk
5ml/1 tsp vanilla extract
115g/4oz plain (semisweet) chocolate
15ml/1 tbsp water
275g/10oz/2¹⁄₂ cups plain
   (all-purpose) flour
5ml/1 tsp baking powder
2.5ml/¹⁄₂ tsp bicarbonate of soda
   (baking soda)

300g/11oz/1¹⁄₂ cups caster
   (superfine) sugar
3 eggs

FOR THE VANILLA ICING

40g/1¹⁄₂ oz/3 tbsp butter
115g/4oz/1 cup icing (confectioners') sugar
2.5ml/¹⁄₂ tsp vanilla extract
15–30ml/1–2 tbsp milk

1 Preheat the oven to 180°C/ 350°F/Gas 4. Arrange 24 paper cases in muffin tins (pans), or grease the cups of the tins.

2 In a large mixing bowl, beat the butter with an electric mixer until it is light and fluffy. Beat in the milk and the vanilla extract.

3 Melt the chocolate with the water in a bowl set over a pan of simmering water, then add to the butter mixture. Sift the flour, baking powder, bicarbonate of soda and sugar over the batter in batches and stir. Add the eggs one at a time, beating well after each addition.

4 Divide the mixture evenly among the muffin cases. Bake for 25 minutes or until a skewer inserted into the centre comes out clean. Cool on a wire rack.

5 For the icing, beat the butter with the icing sugar and vanilla extract. Add enough milk to make a creamy mixture.

6 Spread the icing on top of each of the cooled cakes.

Nutritional information per portion: Energy 210kcal/ 884kJ; Protein 2.5g; Carbohydrate 30.4g, of which sugars 21.6g; Fat 9.7g, of which saturates 5.8g; Cholesterol 44mg; Calcium 39mg; Fibre 0.5g; Sodium 67mg.

Chocolate and vanilla cupcakes

A snowy topping of thick, creamy mascarpone whipped with sugar and flecked with the fragrant black seeds of vanilla conceals a lovely dark chocolate cake.

MAKES 10

100g/3½oz/scant ½ cup caster (superfine) sugar
115g/4oz/1 cup self-raising (self-rising) flour, sifted
3 eggs, lightly beaten
115g/4oz/½ cup butter, melted
50g/2oz/½ cup ground almonds
5ml/1 tsp vanilla extract
50g/2oz dark (bittersweet) chocolate, melted

FOR THE TOPPING

½ vanilla pod (bean)
175g/6oz/¾ cup butter, softened
2.5ml/½ tsp finely grated lemon rind
350g/12oz/3 cups icing (confectioners') sugar, sifted, plus extra for dusting
225g/8oz/1 cup mascarpone

1 Preheat the oven to 180°C/350°F/Gas 4. Line a muffin tin (pan) with 10 paper cases.

2 Mix the sugar with the flour. Stir in the eggs and add the melted butter, ground almonds and vanilla extract, followed by the melted chocolate. Stir together, then cover the bowl and chill for 30 minutes to 1 hour.

3 Spoon the mixture into the muffin cases, filling them three-quarters full. Bake for 25 minutes, or until the cakes are firm. Leave on a wire rack to cool.

4 For the topping, scrape the seeds from the vanilla pod and reserve. Cut the pod into fine strips. In a bowl beat the butter, lemon rind, sugar and mascarpone until smooth. Stir in the vanilla seeds. Pipe on to the cakes. Dust with icing sugar and top with the vanilla strips.

COOK'S TIP

You can store vanilla pods in an airtight container in a dark, cool cupboard for about 2 years.

Nutritional information per portion: Energy 608kcal/ 2537kJ; Protein 5.3g; Carbohydrate 59.6g, of which sugars 50.4g; Fat 40.4g, of which saturates 23.9g; Cholesterol 146mg; Calcium 89mg; Fibre 0.7g; Sodium 310mg.

Vanilla butterfly cakes

These pretty little cakes are filled with a simple vanilla buttercream. The butterfly 'wings' are so easy to make, but when dusted with a little icing sugar make a really elegant decoration.

MAKES 10

175g/6oz/³⁄4 cup butter, softened
175g/6oz/³⁄4 cup caster (superfine) sugar
5ml/1 tsp vanilla extract
4 eggs, lightly beaten
175g/6oz/1¹⁄2 cups self-raising
   (self-rising) flour, sifted

FOR THE FILLING

75g/3oz/6 tbsp butter, softened
175g/6oz/1¹⁄2 cups icing (confectioners')
   sugar, double sifted, plus extra for dusting
¹⁄2 vanilla pod (bean), split, or a few drops
   of vanilla extract

1 Preheat the oven to 180°C/350°F/Gas 4. Line 8–9 cups of a bun tin (pan) with paper cases.

2 Beat the butter and sugar together until light and creamy. Add the vanilla. Gradually add the eggs, beating well after each addition. Add the sifted flour and fold into the mixture until just combined.

3 Divide the mixture among the paper cases and bake for 20 minutes until the cakes are golden brown and the centres feel firm to the touch. Remove from the oven. Leave to cool in the tin for 5 minutes, then transfer the cakes to a wire rack to cool completely.

4 To make the buttercream filling, beat the butter and icing sugar together until smooth. For the best vanilla flavour, split the vanilla pod in half and scrape out the seeds. Discard the pod and mix the seeds into the buttercream. Alternatively, add a few drops of vanilla extract to the mixture.

5 When the cakes have cooled, carefully cut round the lightly domed tops with a small sharp knife and remove the top of each cake. Slice the tops in half to form two semicircles, to make the butterfly wings. Set aside.

6 Use a piping (icing) bag with a star nozzle to pipe a whirl of buttercream into each cake. Press the wings into the cream and dust with sifted icing sugar.

Nutritional information per portion: Energy 455kcal/1905kJ; Protein 4.8g; Carbohydrate 55.3g, of which sugars 40.9g; Fat 25.4g, of which saturates 15.7g; Cholesterol 148mg; Calcium 106mg; Fibre 0.6g; Sodium 312mg.

Carrot cupcakes

These wonderfully tasty cakes are made using an easy all-in-one recipe. The mixture is enriched with grated carrots, which add sweetness as well as keeping the cakes moist and light.

MAKES 8–10

225g/8oz/1 cup caster (superfine) sugar
3 eggs
200ml/7fl oz/scant 1 cup vegetable oil
grated rind and juice of 1 orange
225g/8oz/2 cups self-raising (self-rising)
   wholemeal (whole-wheat) flour
5ml/1 tsp ground cinnamon
2.5ml/½ tsp grated nutmeg
pinch of salt
350g/12oz grated carrot, squeezed dry
175g/6oz/1 cup walnuts, chopped

FOR THE TOPPING

225g/8oz/1 cup cream cheese
30ml/2 tbsp clear honey
15ml/1 tbsp orange juice
50g/2oz marzipan
orange food colouring
small quantity angelica

1 Preheat the oven to 180°C/350°F/ Gas 4. Line a bun tin (pan) with paper cases.

2 Beat the sugar, eggs, oil, orange rind and juice together until light and frothy. Sift in the flour, spices and salt and beat for a further minute. Stir in the carrots and nuts.

3 Fill the prepared paper cases and bake for 25 minutes, until the cakes are firm in the centre. Turn out on to a wire rack to cool.

4 For the icing, beat the cheese, honey and orange juice together. Chill for 30 minutes. Tint the marzipan orange with food colouring.

5 Break off small pieces and roll between your palms to form carrot shapes. Using a knife, press marks around the carrots and stick small pieces of angelica in the tops to resemble stalks.

6 Spread the icing over the tops of the cooled cakes. Arrange the carrots on the cakes.

Nutritional information per portion: Energy 542kcal/2258kJ; Protein 7.9g; Carbohydrate 46.9g, of which sugars 32.7g; Fat 37.1g, of which saturates 9.6g; Cholesterol 78mg; Calcium 75mg; Fibre 3.4g; Sodium 102mg.

Autumn cupcakes

Small leaves made from rolled-out marzipan can make stunning cake decorations, used by themselves or combined with crystallized or sugarpaste flowers.

MAKES 10

2 eggs
115g/4oz/½ cup caster (superfine) sugar
50ml/2fl oz/¼ cup double
    (heavy) cream
finely grated rind of 1 lemon
115g/4oz/1 cup self-raising
    (self-rising) flour
2.5ml/½ tsp baking powder
50g/2oz/4 tbsp butter, melted

FOR THE TOPPING

225g/8oz/2 cups icing
    (confectioners') sugar
15–30ml/1–2 tbsp hot water

FOR THE DECORATION

50g/2oz marzipan, tinted as desired

1 Preheat the oven to 180°C/350°F/ Gas 4 and line 10 holes of a bun tin (pan) with paper cases. Beat the eggs with the sugar. Beat in the cream for 1 minute, then add the lemon rind.

2 Sift the flour with the baking powder, then fold it lightly into the mixture, followed by the butter. Three-quarters fill the paper cases with the cake mixture. Bake in the centre of the oven for 15 minutes until risen and golden brown.

3 Remove from the oven and leave to cool in the bun tin for 5 minutes, then transfer the cakes to a wire rack to cool completely.

4 To make the leaves, roll out the marzipan thinly. Cut out leaves with a cutter, or cut round a card template with a knife. Leave to dry on baking parchment. Paint the veins and edges with food colouring using a brush.

5 To make the icing, sift the icing sugar into a bowl, then gradually mix in the water, a few drops at a time, beating until the mixture is the consistency of cream.

6 Use the icing to cover the cakes, while it is smooth and fluid. Before the icing dries, carefully arrange the leaves on top of the cakes.

Nutritional information per portion: Energy 267kcal/1129kJ; Protein 2.9g; Carbohydrate 48g, of which sugars 39.2g; Fat 8.7g, of which saturates 4.6g; Cholesterol 56mg; Calcium 46mg; Fibre 0.5g; Sodium 57mg.

Valentine cupcakes

Pink and white sugared hearts make a classic cake decoration that's very easy to achieve, using a few cutters in different sizes. Mix and match the colours and designs for a contemporary twist.

MAKES 10

175g/6oz/¾ cup butter, softened
175g/6oz/¾ cup caster (superfine) sugar
4 eggs, lightly beaten
5ml/1 tsp vanilla extract
175g/6oz/1½ cups self-raising
    (self-rising) flour, sifted

FOR THE TOPPING

350g/12oz icing (confectioners') sugar,
    sifted
115g/4oz white sugarpaste
pink food colouring
pink candy sugar or sprinkles

Nutritional information per portion: Energy 501kcal/
2109kJ; Protein 5g; Carbohydrate 83.6g, of which sugars
68.8g; Fat 18.6g, of which saturates 11.2g; Cholesterol
129mg; Calcium 78mg; Fibre 0.6g; Sodium 181mg.

1 Preheat the oven to 180°C/350°F/ Gas 4. Line the cups of a bun tin (pan) with paper cases.

2 Beat the butter and sugar until light and creamy. Add the beaten eggs and beat well after each addition. Stir in the vanilla extract. Add the flour and fold in.

3 Spoon the mixture into the paper cases. Bake for 20 minutes until golden. Leave on a wire rack to cool.

4 For the topping, mix the sugar with enough hot water to make a thick icing. Divide between two bowls and tint one pink. Spread on to the cakes.

5 Cut out heart shapes in different shades of pink sugarpaste. Paint some with water and cover with candy sugar or sprinkles. When dry, stick on to the cakes.

Mini party cakes

Once these pretty party cakes are iced, a sherbet 'flying saucer' sweet is stuck on top of each one, before being decorated with butterflies and flowers.

MAKES 48 TINY CAKES

175g/6oz/³⁄₄ cup butter, softened
175g/6oz/³⁄₄ cup caster (superfine) sugar
4 eggs, lightly beaten
5ml/1 tsp vanilla extract
175g/6oz/1¹⁄₂ cups self-raising (self-rising) flour, sifted

FOR THE ICING AND DECORATIONS

150g/5oz/1¹⁄₄ cups icing (confectioners') sugar, sifted
food colouring in 4 colours
115g/4oz white sugarpaste
sherbet-filled flying saucer sweets (candies)

1 Preheat the oven to 180°C/350°F/ Gas 4. Line the cups of four 12-cup mini cupcake trays with paper cases.

2 Beat the butter and sugar until light and creamy. Gradually add the eggs and beat well after each addition. Add the vanilla and flour and fold into the butter mixture until just combined.

3 Half-fill the paper cases and bake for 12 minutes until golden. Leave on a wire rack to cool completely.

4 Make the icing with just enough hot water (about 20ml/4 tsp) to make a soft glacé icing. Divide the icing between four bowls, then tint each with a different food colour, keeping the colours pale.

5 Ice each cake. Decorate flying saucer sweets with tinted sprinkles and sugarpaste flowers, leaves and butterflies. Attach with glacé icing. Stick each to the top of a cupcake with glacé icing.

Nutritional information per portion: Energy 78kcal/329kJ; Protein 0.9g; Carbohydrate 11.6g, of which sugars 8.9g; Fat 3.5g, of which saturates 2.1g; Cholesterol 24mg; Calcium 20mg; Fibre 0.1g; Sodium 47mg.

Christmas spice cupcakes

Mincemeat, brandy and freshly ground spices are the main ingredients in these delicious celebration cupcakes, which are ideal for those who love the rich spicy flavours of Christmas.

MAKES 14

2 eggs
115g/4oz/½ cup golden caster
   (superfine) sugar
50ml/2fl oz/¼ cup double (heavy) cream
grated rind of 1 clementine
115g/4oz/⅓ cup mincemeat
115g/4oz/1 cup self-raising
   (self-rising) flour
2.5ml/½ tsp baking powder
5ml/1 tsp mixed (apple pie) spice
10ml/2 tsp brandy
50g/2oz/4 tbsp butter, melted

FOR THE DECORATION

350g/12oz/3 cups icing (confectioners')
   sugar, sifted
15ml/1 tbsp hot water
red food colouring
175g/6oz sugarpaste

1 Preheat the oven to 180°C/350°F/Gas 4. Line the cups of a bun tin (pan) with paper cases.

2 Lightly beat the eggs with the sugar. Beat the cream into the egg mixture for about 1 minute, then add the grated clementine rind. Fold in the mincemeat. Sift in the flour, baking powder and mixed spice and fold in. Finally add the brandy and the melted butter and stir to combine.

3 Half-fill the paper cases with the batter. Place in the centre of the oven and bake for 15 minutes until risen and golden. Leave on a wire rack to cool.

4 To make the icing, mix the sugar with just enough hot water to make a soft icing. Tint one-third of it with the red food colour and spoon over four of the cakes. Ice the remaining cakes with the white icing.

5 Set aside one-third of the sugarpaste and colour the rest red. Roll both out and stamp out 10 red and 4 white snowflakes. Stick one on each cake before the icing sets.

Nutritional information per portion: Energy 272kcal/1153kJ; Protein 2g; Carbohydrate 56g, of which sugars 49.7g; Fat 6.1g, of which saturates 3.4g; Cholesterol 40mg; Calcium 43mg; Fibre 0.4g; Sodium 52mg.

Almond cupcakes with grapes

Bunches of marzipan grapes decorate these spectacular tea party cakes, but if you would prefer a simpler decoration you could finish the cakes elegantly with just a single green vine leaf laid on top.

MAKES 10

225g/8oz marzipan
75g/3oz/6 tbsp butter, softened
100g/3½oz/scant ½ cup caster
    (superfine) sugar
3 eggs, lightly beaten
15ml/1 tbsp grappa
100g/3½oz/scant ½ cup
    ground almonds
150g/5oz/1¼ cups plain
    (all-purpose) flour
10ml/2 tsp baking powder
10ml/2 tsp Seville orange marmalade,
    sieved (strained)

FOR THE DECORATION
500g/1¼ lb white marzipan
green and purple food colouring
50g/2oz royal icing
a little sieved (strained) apricot jam
10 dried or fresh apple stalks (optional)

1 Preheat the oven to 180°C/350°F/Gas 4. Line the cups of a bun tin (pan) with paper cases. Beat the marzipan, butter and sugar together until smooth with an electric mixer. With the whisk running, add the eggs in a very thin stream, beating well until the mixture is very smooth. Fold in the grappa, almonds and flour sifted with the baking powder. Finally, stir in the marmalade.

2 Fill the paper cases just over half full with the mixture and bake for 20 minutes until golden and springy to the touch in the centre. Leave to cool completely on a wire rack, then slice off the cake tops level with the tops of the cases.

3 Roll out 175g/6oz marzipan fairly thinly on a board dusted with icing sugar. Using a crinkle-edged cutter, cut 10 circles. Colour 115g/4oz marzipan apple green. Roll it out thinly and cut out 10 vine leaves. Colour the remaining marzipan purple and roll it into nine smooth balls for each cake.

4 Heat the jam and brush on each cake. Press on the circles of marzipan. Brush the centre of each circle with jam and stick on the grapes, then attach a vine leaf with royal icing and push in an apple stalk, if using.

Nutritional information per portion: Energy 572kcal/2404kJ; Protein 10.5g; Carbohydrate 76.9g, of which sugars 65g; Fat 25.7g, of which saturates 6.1g; Cholesterol 81mg; Calcium 122mg; Fibre 2.9g; Sodium 94mg.

Orange blossom whoopie pies

This delightful, zesty and citrusy whoopie pie, with a light and fragrant honey buttercream filling, can be made a few days in advance to allow all the flavours to completely infuse.

MAKES 12 WHOOPIE PIES

FOR THE CAKES
130g/4¹/₂oz/generous ¹/₂ cup unsalted
    butter, softened
150g/5oz/³/₄ cup caster (superfine) sugar
seeds of 1 vanilla pod (bean)
1 egg
325g/11¹/₂oz/scant 3 cups plain
    (all-purpose) flour
7.5ml/1¹/₂ tsp bicarbonate of soda
    (baking soda)
5ml/1 tsp salt
finely grated rind of 1 orange
150ml/¹/₄ pint/²/₃ cup buttermilk
50ml/2fl oz/¹/₄ cup milk
10ml/2 tsp orange flower water

FOR THE FILLING
2 egg whites
125g/4¹/₄oz/generous ¹/₂ cup caster
    (superfine) sugar
225g/8oz/1 cup unsalted butter
finely grated rind and juice of ¹/₂ orange
5ml/1 tsp orange flower water
15ml/1 tbsp clear honey

**FOR THE ICING AND
DECORATION**
150g/5oz/1¹/₄ cups icing
    (confectioners') sugar
25ml/1¹/₂ tbsp orange juice
grated orange rind and mini sweets
    (candies), to decorate

Nutritional information per portion: Energy 486kcal/
2052kJ; Protein 4g; Carbohydrate 63g, of which sugars
42g; Fat 26g, of which saturates 16g; Cholesterol 88mg;
Calcium 69mg; Fibre 1.0g; Sodium 335mg.

1 Preheat the oven to 180°C/350°F/ Gas 4. Line two baking trays with baking parchment. Whisk the butter, sugar and vanilla seeds in a bowl until fluffy. Whisk in the egg.

2 In a separate bowl, sift the flour, bicarbonate of soda and salt. Add the orange rind. In a measuring jug (cup), mix the buttermilk, milk and orange flower water. Fold half of the dry ingredients into the butter mixture. Add the buttermilk mixture, then the rest of the dry ingredients.

3 Using a piping (pastry) bag fitted with a large plain nozzle, pipe 12 5cm/2in rounds of cake mixture (batter) about 5cm/2in apart on each baking tray. Bake for 12–15 minutes. Transfer to a wire rack.

4 Using an electric whisk, whisk the egg whites and sugar in a heatproof bowl over a pan of simmering water, until the mixture is white and hot. Remove from the heat and whisk on high until cool. On low, gradually whisk in the butter. Add the rind, juice, orange flower water and honey.

5 Mix the icing sugar and juice. Using a star-shaped nozzle, pipe filling on to the flat side of one cake and top with another. Repeat to make 12, then decorate the pies.

Mango passion whoopie pies

Exotic and enticing, these whoopie pies are filled with mango pieces and topped with passion fruit. They are also good with other tropical fruits, such as papaya and star fruit (carambola).

MAKES 12 WHOOPIE PIES

FOR THE CAKES

130g/4¹/₂oz/generous ¹/₂ cup unsalted butter, softened

150g/5oz/³/₄ cup caster (superfine) sugar

seeds of 1 vanilla pod (bean)

1 egg

325g/11¹/₂oz/scant 3 cups plain (all-purpose) flour

7.5ml/1¹/₂ tsp bicarbonate of soda (baking soda)

5ml/1 tsp salt

150ml/¹/₄ pint/²/₃ cup buttermilk

50ml/2fl oz/¹/₄ cup milk

FOR THE FILLING

200ml/7fl oz/scant 1 cup double (heavy) cream

seeds of 1 vanilla pod (bean)

25g/1oz/2 tbsp caster (superfine) sugar

¹/₂ mango, peeled, stoned (pitted) and finely chopped

FOR THE GLAZE

90ml/6 tbsp icing (confectioners') sugar

juice of 2 passion fruits

pulp of 3 passion fruits, including seeds, to decorate

1 Preheat the oven to 180°C/350°F/Gas 4. Line two baking trays with baking parchment or silicone mats. For the cakes, whisk the butter, sugar and vanilla seeds until fluffy. Whisk in the egg.

2 In a separate bowl, sift the flour with the bicarbonate of soda and salt. Fold half of the dry ingredients into the butter mixture. Mix in the buttermilk and milk, then the remainder of the dry ingredients.

3 Using a piping (pastry) bag fitted with a large plain nozzle, pipe 12 5cm/2in rounds of mixture (batter) 5cm/2in apart on each baking tray. Bake for 12–15 minutes, or until the cakes bounce back when pressed. Transfer to a wire rack to cool.

4 For the filling, put the cream, vanilla seeds and sugar in a bowl and whisk until stiff peaks form. Fold in the chopped mango.

5 To make the glaze, mix the icing sugar and passion fruit juice until smooth and syrupy.

6 Place a tablespoonful of the filling on to the flat side of one cake and top with the flat side of another.

7 Repeat to make 12 pies. Spread glaze over the top of each pie, then decorate with passion fruit pulp.

Nutritional information per portion: Energy 363kcal/1526kJ; Protein 4g; Carbohydrate 47g, of which sugars 26g; Fat 19g, of which saturates 12g; Cholesterol 98mg; Calcium 74mg; Fibre 1.2g; Sodium 325mg.

Banoffee and walnut whoopie pies

Banoffee pie is a classic flavour combination, which is ideal for those with a sweet tooth. However, whipped cream for the filling balances the sweetness of the caramel.

MAKES 12 WHOOPIE PIES

FOR THE CAKES

130g/4½oz/generous ½ cup unsalted
   butter, softened
150g/5oz/generous ½ cup soft light
   brown sugar
1 egg, beaten
300g/11oz/2¾ cups plain
   (all-purpose) flour
7.5ml/1½ tsp bicarbonate of soda
   (baking soda)
5ml/1 tsp salt
2.5ml/½ tsp ground cinnamon

a pinch of freshly grated nutmeg
50ml/2fl oz/¼ cup milk
150ml/¼ pint/⅔ cup buttermilk
200g/7oz mashed bananas
40g/1½oz/scant ½ cup walnuts,
   roughly chopped

FOR THE FILLING

150ml/¼ pint/⅔ cup double
   (heavy) cream
100g/3¾oz dulce de leche

1 Preheat the oven to 180°C/350°F/ Gas 4. Line two baking trays with baking parchment or silicone mats.

2 For the cakes, whisk the butter and brown sugar together until light and fluffy. Whisk in the egg.

3 In a separate bowl, sift the flour with the bicarbonate of soda, salt, cinnamon and nutmeg. Fold half of the dry ingredients into the butter mixture. Mix in the milk and buttermilk, then the remainder of the dry ingredients. Mix in the mashed bananas and walnuts.

4 Using an ice cream scoop, scoop 12 5cm/2in rounds of cake mixture (batter) 5cm/2in apart on each baking tray. Bake for 12–15 minutes, or until the cakes bounce back when pressed. Transfer to a wire rack.

5 To make the filling, whip the cream until stiff peaks form. Fold in the dulce de leche. Using a piping (pastry) bag fitted with a star-shaped nozzle, pipe some whipped cream filling on to the flat side of one cake and top with the flat side of another. Repeat to make 12 pies.

Nutritional information per portion: Energy 382kcal/ -1604kJ; Protein 6g; Carbohydrate 46g, of which sugars 27g; Fat 21g, of which saturates 12g; Cholesterol 68mg; Calcium 127mg; Fibre 1.6g; Sodium 349mg.

Christmas cake whoopie pies

These whoopie pies are flavoursome and festive, bursting with fruit and spices. With their spicy ingredients and red and silver balls, they embody all the joy of a Christmas cake in a few bites.

MAKES 12 WHOOPIE PIES

FOR THE CAKES

125g/4¼oz/8½ tbsp unsalted
   butter, softened
175g/6oz/¾ cup soft light brown sugar
seeds of 1 vanilla pod (bean)
1 egg
300g/11oz/2¾ cups plain
   (all-purpose) flour
7.5ml/1½ tsp bicarbonate of soda
   (baking soda)
5ml/1 tsp salt
2.5ml/½ tsp ground mixed
   (apple pie) spice
2.5ml/½ tsp ground cinnamon
finely grated rind of 1 orange
finely grated rind of 1 lemon
250ml/8fl oz/1 cup buttermilk
100g/3¾oz/⅔ cup mixed dried fruit

**FOR THE MARSHMALLOW
FILLING**

50ml/2fl oz/¼ cup boiling water
15ml/1 tbsp powdered gelatine
175g/6oz/generous ¾ cup caster
   (superfine) sugar
75ml/2½fl oz/⅓ cup golden (light
   corn) syrup
25ml/1½ tbsp cold water

FOR THE TOPPING

100ml/3½fl oz/scant
   ½ cup brandy
150g/5oz/1¼ cups royal icing
   (confectioners') sugar
25ml/1½ tbsp cold water
red and silver edible balls,
   to decorate

1 Preheat the oven to 180°C/350°F/ Gas 4. Line two baking trays with baking parchment. For the cakes, whisk the butter, sugar and vanilla until fluffy. Whisk in the egg.

2 In a separate bowl, sift the flour with the bicarbonate of soda, salt and ground spices, then add the citrus rinds. Fold half of the dry ingredients into the butter mixture. Mix in the buttermilk, the rest of the dry ingredients and the dried fruit.

3 Using a piping (pastry) bag fitted with a large plain nozzle, pipe 12 5cm/2in rounds of cake mixture (batter) 5cm/2in apart on each baking tray. Bake for 12–15 minutes. Cool on a wire rack.

4 For the marshmallow, sprinkle the the gelatine over the boiling water in the bowl of an electric mixer.

5 Whisk until the gelatine dissolves. Set aside. Bring the sugar, golden syrup and water to a boil. With the mixer on low, pour the hot sugar syrup into the bowl. Whisk on high for 5 minutes. Spoon some filling on to the flat side of one cake and top with another. Repeat to make 12 pies.

6 Drizzle warmed brandy over the pies. Leave to dry while you make the icing. Mix the royal icing sugar with the water to a paste. Spread on the tops of the pies, using a cocktail stick (toothpick) to create a snowy texture. Decorate with red and silver balls.

Nutritional information per portion: Energy 412kcal/ 1746kJ; Protein 4g; Carbohydrate 78g, of which sugars 59g; Fat 10g, of which saturates 6g; Cholesterol 44mg; Calcium 85mg; Fibre 1.7g; Sodium 350mg.

Mini Victoria sponge pops

The Victoria sponge is one of England's most popular teatime treats – light vanilla cakes sandwiched together with buttercream and jam, and elegantly dusted with icing sugar. These mini versions are perfect for serving with a pot of freshly brewed tea for an afternoon tea party.

MAKES 10

FOR THE CAKES
50g/2oz/¼ cup butter, softened
50g/2oz/¼ cup caster (superfine) sugar
1 egg
5ml/1 tsp vanilla extract
50g/2oz/½ cup self-raising (self-rising) flour, sifted
5ml/1 tsp baking powder

FOR THE BUTTERCREAM AND JAM FILLING
100g/3¾oz/scant 1 cup icing (confectioners') sugar, plus extra for dusting
30g/1¼oz/2½ tbsp butter, softened
30g/1¼oz/scant ¼ cup cream cheese
5ml/1 tsp vanilla extract
a little milk, for mixing (optional)
60–75ml/4–5 tbsp good quality strawberry jam

TO SERVE
10 lollipop sticks
10 tiny ribbons (optional)

1 Preheat the oven to 180°C/350°F/ Gas 4. Grease a 10-cup straight-sided mini muffin tin (pan). Cream the butter and sugar until fluffy. Beat in the egg and vanilla extract.

2 Sift the flour and baking powder into the butter mixture, then fold in. Divide the cake mixture (batter) between the cups of the prepared tin. Bake for 12–15 minutes or until the cakes spring back when pressed.. Transfer to a wire rack to cool.

3 For the buttercream, sift the icing sugar into a bowl, add the butter, cream cheese and vanilla extract, and whisk for 3 minutes, or until creamy. Add a little milk if needed.

4 Cut each of the cakes in half horizontally. Using a piping (pastry) bag fitted with a small star-shaped nozzle, pipe the buttercream on to the bottom half of each cake.

5 With a teaspoon, add strawberry jam to each. Top with the other cake halves and dust with icing sugar. Insert a lollipop stick into the top of each cake and tie a ribbon around it.

Nutritional information per portion: Energy 177kcal/ 742kJ; Protein 2g; Carbohydrate 24g, of which sugars 20g; Fat 9g, of which saturates 5g; Cholesterol 45mg; Calcium 33mg; Fibre 0.3g; Sodium 136mg.

Red velvet pops

Red velvet cake is an all-time American classic. Dainty cupcakes are coloured red and flavoured with cocoa to give them their distinctive look and taste. Each cupcake is topped with a swirl of cream cheese icing which has a lovely sharpness to complement the sweet sponge cake.

MAKES 20

FOR THE CAKES

50g/2oz/¼ cup butter, softened
50g/2oz/¼ cup caster (superfine) sugar
1 egg
45g/1¾oz/scant ½ cup self-raising
   (self-rising) flour, sifted
15g/½oz unsweetened cocoa powder,
   sifted, plus extra for dusting
15ml/1 tbsp buttermilk
a few drops of red food colouring gel

FOR THE CREAM CHEESE ICING

200g/7oz/1¾ cups icing
   (confectioners') sugar
50g/2oz white chocolate, melted
   and cooled
30g/1¼oz/scant ¼ cup cream cheese
15ml/1 tbsp buttermilk

TO SERVE

20 wooden skewers
20 mini marshmallows (optional)

1 Preheat the oven to 180°C/ 350°F/Gas 4. Grease a 24-cup mini muffin tin (pan). To make the cakes, cream the butter and caster sugar together until light and fluffy, then beat in the egg.

2 Sift the flour and cocoa powder together in a separate bowl, then fold into the butter mixture with the buttermilk.

3 Add a few drops of red food colouring gel (enough to colour the mixture an even reddish brown).

4 Divide the cake mixture (batter) among 20 cups of the prepared mini muffin tin. Bake for 12–15 minutes, or until the cakes spring back when pressed. Transfer to a wire rack.

5 For the icing, sift the icing sugar into a bowl, add the white chocolate, cream cheese and buttermilk, and whisk for 3 minutes, or until creamy.

6 Using a piping (pastry) bag fitted with a large star-shaped nozzle, pipe a swirl of icing on top of each cake. Dust with a little sifted cocoa powder and, when ready to serve, insert a wooden skewer into the base of each cake, securing with a mini marshmallow, if necessary.

Nutritional information per portion: Energy 103kcal/ 433 kJ; Protein 1g; Carbohydrate 16g, of which sugars 15g; Fat 4g, of which saturates 2g; Cholesterol 20mg, Calcium 22mg; Fibre 0.1g; Sodium 44mg.

Rocky road pops

These rich pops take their inspiration from rocky road ice cream and are packed with cherries, chocolate, marshmallows and cookies to give an added crunch.

MAKES 28

FOR THE CHOCOLATE SLICE
400g/14oz plain (semisweet)
    chocolate, chopped
125g/4¼oz/8½ tbsp butter
100g/3¾oz/scant 2 cups digestive
    biscuits (graham crackers), crushed
100g/3¾oz/scant 2 cups chocolate
    sandwich cookies, crushed
75g/3oz mini marshmallows
150g/5oz/scant ¾ cup glacé (candied)
    cherries, halved

FOR THE TOPPING
100g/3¾oz/scant ½ cup glacé
    (candied) cherries, halved
50g/2oz mini marshmallows
100g/3¾oz white chocolate, melted

TO SERVE
28 wooden skewers

1 Grease and line a 28 x 18cm/11 x 7in deep rectangular cake tin (pan).

2 To make the chocolate slice, place the chocolate and butter in a large heatproof bowl set over a pan of simmering water, taking care that the water does not touch the bottom of the bowl. Stir until the butter and chocolate are melted and blended, then remove from the heat.

3 Add all the remaining ingredients for the chocolate slice to the bowl and mix well to coat everything in the chocolate. Spoon the mixture into the tin and press out flat using a spoon.

4 For the topping, sprinkle the glacé cherries and mini marshmallows over the top. Drizzle over the white chocolate in thin lines using a spoon. Leave to set in the refrigerator.

5 To serve, remove the slice from the tin and cut into 28 squares. Insert a wooden skewer into each square.

Nutritional information per portion: Energy 196kcal/821kJ; Protein 2g; Carbohydrate 26g, of which sugars 22g; Fat 10g, of which saturates 6g; Cholesterol 14mg; Calcium 27mg; Fibre 0.3g; Sodium 62mg.

Black Forest cherry pops

The German Black Forest gateau is popular worldwide, and these mini versions would make fun canapés to serve at any party. Whipped cream from a spray can is the perfect topping.

MAKES 30

FOR THE CAKES
115g/4oz/½ cup butter, softened
115g/4oz/generous ½ cup caster (superfine) sugar
2 eggs
115g/4oz/1 cup self-raising (self-rising) flour
2.5ml/½ tsp vanilla extract
90g/3½oz cherry compote
75ml/2½fl oz/⅓ cup low-fat natural (plain) yogurt

FOR THE CHOCOLATE GANACHE
200g/7oz plain (semisweet) chocolate, chopped
105ml/7 tbsp double (heavy) cream
25g/1oz/2 tbsp butter, softened

TO DECORATE AND SERVE
a spray can of whipped cream, 30 fresh cherries, chocolate 'spaghetti' curls, to sprinkle and 30 lollipop sticks, to serve

1 Preheat the oven to 180°C/350°F/Gas 4. Grease a 30-cup mini muffin tin (pan).

2 For the cakes, cream the butter and sugar together until light and fluffy. Beat in the eggs. Sift in the flour and fold in with the vanilla extract, cherry compote and yogurt. Divide the cake mixture (batter) among the cups of the prepared tin; about a heaped teaspoon in each. Bake for 15–18 minutes, until the cakes spring back when pressed. Transfer to a wire rack to cool. Once cool, insert a stick into the base of each cake.

3 To prepare the chocolate ganache, place the chocolate, cream and butter in a heatproof bowl set over a pan of simmering water, taking care that the water does not touch the bottom of the bowl. Stir until the sauce is smooth, and glossy. Remove from the heat.

4 Dip the top of each cake into the ganache, then insert the sticks into a foam block and leave the cake pops to set. Squirt a little spray cream on to each cake, top with a cherry and sprinkle with chocolate spaghetti curls.

Nutritional information per portion: Energy 150kcal/624kJ; Protein 2g; Carbohydrate 13g, of which sugars 10g; Fat 10g, of which saturates 6g; Cholesterol 36mg; Calcium 29mg; Fibre 0.2g; Sodium 52mg.

Mini chocolate Sachertortes

The Hotel Sacher in Vienna is said to be the original home of the ultimate Austrian delight, the Sachertorte. It is a rich chocolate and hazelnut cake covered in a chocolate ganache.

MAKES 24

FOR THE CAKES
225g/8oz/1 cup butter, softened
225g/8oz/generous 1 cup caster (superfine) sugar
4 eggs
175g/6oz/1½ cups self-raising (self-rising) flour
125g/4¼oz/generous 1 cup ground hazelnuts
100g/3¾oz dark (bittersweet) chocolate, melted
10ml/2 tsp vanilla extract
30ml/2 tbsp apricot jam
30ml/2 tbsp crème fraîche

FOR THE APRICOT GLAZE
90ml/6 tbsp apricot jam
juice of 2 lemons

FOR THE GANACHE
200g/7oz dark (bittersweet) chocolate, chopped
30g/1¼oz/2½ tbsp butter
120ml/4fl oz/½ cup double (heavy) cream

TO DECORATE AND SERVE
chocolate sprinkles
24 paper cake cases, to serve
24 small forks, to serve

Nutritional information per portion: Energy 221kcal/ 923kJ; Protein 3g; Carbohydrate 22g, of which sugars 17g; Fat 14g, of which saturates 6g; Cholesterol 60mg; Calcium 44mg; Fibre 0.8g; Sodium 101mg.

1 Preheat the oven to 180°C/350°F/ Gas 4. Grease and line two 20cm/ 8in square cake tins (pans). Cream the butter and sugar, beat in the eggs, then sift in the flour and fold it in with the hazelnuts, chocolate, vanilla extract, jam and crème fraîche.

2 Divide the cake mixture (batter) between the tins and level the tops. Bake for 30–35 minutes, until firm to the touch. Leave the cakes to cool, then turn out and cut out 24 rounds with a 5cm/2in round cutter.

3 For the glaze, melt the jam and lemon juice over gentle heat. Press the mixture through a sieve (strainer). Roll the sides of each cake in the glaze, then dip in the top. Leave on a wire rack for 20 minutes.

4 For the ganache, put the chocolate, butter and cream (reserving 15ml/1 tbsp cream) in a bowl over a pan of simmering water. Stir to form a smooth sauce. Remove from the heat, cool slightly, then add the reserved cream. When thick, spread around the edges of each cake, then leave to set. Place a spoonful of ganache on top of each.

5 Add sprinkles. Once set, put the cakes in a paper cases and insert a small fork into the top of each cake.

Triple chocolate brownie pops

Rich, indulgent brownie pops are perfect for any occasion – dipped in melted white chocolate and decorated with brightly coloured sugar sprinkles, these are a chocolate lover's dream!

MAKES 24

FOR THE BROWNIES
250g/9oz/generous 1 cup butter
350g/12oz plain (semisweet) chocolate, roughly chopped
250g/9oz/scant 1⅓ cups caster (superfine) sugar
250g/9oz/generous 1 cup soft dark brown sugar
5 eggs
5ml/1 tsp vanilla extract
200g/7oz/1¾ cups plain (all-purpose) flour, sifted
200g/7oz white chocolate chips

TO DECORATE AND SERVE
24 lollipop sticks
150g/5oz white chocolate, melted
coloured sugar sprinkles and chocolate sprinkles

1 Preheat the oven to 180°C/350°F/Gas 4. Grease and line a 30 × 20cm/12 × 8in deep baking tin (pan).

2 For the brownies, put the butter and plain chocolate in a heatproof bowl set over a pan of simmering water. Stir until melted and mixed Remove from the heat and cool.

3 Using an electric hand mixer or whisk, whisk the caster sugar, brown sugar, eggs and vanilla extract in a large bowl until the mixture is very light and has doubled in volume.

4 While you continue to whisk, slowly pour in the cooled melted chocolate mixture, whisking until fully incorporated.

5 Sift in the flour and fold into the chocolate mixture with the chocolate chips. Pour the brownie mixture (batter) into the tin.

6 Bake for 25–35 minutes, or until it has formed a crust and the tip of a sharp knife inserted into the centre comes out clean.

7 Leave the brownie to cool completely in the tin. Once cool, turn out on to a clean work surface or board. Cut out 24 rounds of brownie using a 5cm/2in round cutter.

8 Insert a stick into each brownie. To decorate, dip each brownie pop into the melted white chocolate, then decorate with sprinkles and leave to set before serving.

Nutritional information per portion: Energy 295kcal/1235kJ; Protein 4g; Carbohydrate 33g, of which sugars 26g; Fat 17g, of which saturates 10g; Cholesterol 72mg; Calcium 65mg; Fibre 0.3g; Sodium 58mg.

Birthday cake pops

These pleasing little cakes, holding mini candles, make an unusual centrepiece for a birthday celebration. Purple icing, vanilla buttercream and sprinkles add to their charm.

MAKES 10

FOR THE CAKES
50g/2oz/¼ cup butter, softened
50g/2oz/¼ cup caster (superfine) sugar
1 egg
50g/2oz/½ cup self-raising
   (self-rising) flour
5ml/1 tsp vanilla extract
15ml/1 tbsp sour cream

FOR THE FONDANT ICING
200g/7oz/1¾ cups fondant icing
   (confectioners') sugar, sifted
45–60ml/3–4 tbsp water
a few drops of purple food colouring gel

FOR THE BUTTERCREAM ICING
90g/3½oz/¾ cup icing (confectioners')
   sugar, sifted
30g/1¼oz/2½ tbsp butter, softened
15ml/1 tbsp milk

TO DECORATE AND SERVE
coloured sugar sprinkles
10 mini candles, cut to 1cm/½in, and
   candle holders
10 wooden skewers
10 mini marshmallows

1 Preheat the oven to 180°C/350°F/ Gas 4. Grease a 10-cup straight-sided mini muffin tin (pan). For the cakes, cream the butter and caster sugar until fluffy. Beat in the egg. Sift in the flour and fold in with the vanilla extract and sour cream. Divide the mixture between the cups of the prepared tin. Bake for 12–15 minutes, or until the cakes are golden brown and spring back when gently pressed. Transfer to a wire rack to cool.

2 For the fondant icing, put the fondant icing sugar and water in a bowl with the purple food colouring gel and whisk to a smooth thin icing. Place a sheet of foil under the wire rack. Dip each cake into the icing so that it is coated. Return to the wire rack and leave to set.

3 For the buttercream, sift the icing sugar into a bowl, add the butter and half of the milk. Whisk for 3 minutes. With a star-shaped nozzle, pipe stars around the top of each cake. Decorate with sprinkles. Add a mini candle in a holder. Insert a skewer into the base of each cake, securing with a mini marshmallow.

Nutritional information per portion: Energy 223kcal/ 940kJ; Protein 1g; Carbohydrate 40g, of which sugars 36g; Fat 8g, of which saturates 5g; Cholesterol 41mg; Calcium 22mg; Fibre 0.2g; Sodium 80mg.

Wedding cake pops

These delicate mini tiered wedding cakes make perfect favours at a wedding. The rich vanilla sponge truffles, decorated to look like a full-sized wedding cake, would delight any bride.

MAKES 16

FOR THE CAKES

95g/3¾oz/scant ½ cup
    butter, softened
50g/2oz/¼ cup caster (superfine) sugar
1 egg
50g/2oz/½ cup self-raising
    (self-rising) flour
10ml/2 tsp vanilla extract
90g/3½oz/scant ½ cup cream cheese
16 wooden skewers

**FOR THE DECORATION AND
BUTTERCREAM ICING**

200g/7oz white chocolate, melted
100g/3¾oz/scant 1 cup icing
    (confectioners') sugar
30g/1¼oz/2½ tbsp butter, softened
about 15ml/1 tbsp milk
a few drops of pink food colouring gel
16 sugar flowers and edible glitter,
    to decorate

1 Preheat the oven to 180°C/ 350°F/ Gas 4. Grease and line a 20cm/8in square cake tin (pan).

2 For the cakes, cream 50g/2oz/¼ cup butter and the sugar together until light and fluffy. Beat in the egg. Sift in the flour and fold in with 5ml/1 tsp vanilla extract. Spoon the cake mixture (batter) into the cake tin and level the surface. Bake for 15–20 minutes, until a skewer comes out clean when inserted.

3 Cool in the tin for a few minutes, then transfer to a wire rack. Process the cake to crumbs in a food processor. Transfer to a bowl, add the remaining butter, cream cheese and vanilla extract and mix.

4 Shape the mixture to make 16 each 4cm/1½in cylindrical discs, 2.5cm/1in discs and 1cm/½in discs. Stack one of each disc in towers to create 16 mini wedding cakes. Chill in the freezer for 30 minutes.

5 Remove the cakes from the freezer and press a wooden skewer into the base of each one.

6 To decorate, dip each into the chocolate, to coat. Press the skewers into a foam block and leave to set.

7 For the buttercream icing, sift the icing sugar into a bowl and add the butter and milk. Whisk for 3 minutes, add more milk if necessary. Add the pink colouring.

8 Using a piping (pastry) bag fitted with a small star-shaped nozzle, pipe stars on each tier. Top each with a sugar flower, fixing with melted chocolate, and sprinkle with glitter.

Nutritional information per portion: Energy 213Kcal/ 891kJ; Protein 2g; Carbohydrate 22g, of which sugars 20g; Fat 13g, of which saturates 8g; Cholesterol 37mg; Calcium 56mg; Fibre 0.1g; Sodium 96mg.

Cake Basics

Before you start making cakes, it is good to have a knowledge of what you might need for successful baking. This section guides you through the basic ingredients and flavourings, as well as equipment, and has useful tips to help you to get it right. Cake-making methods are described, as well as cooking tips. Lastly, there are recipes and techniques for toppings so you can embellish your handiwork.

Essential ingredients

Fat, sugar, flour and eggs are the ingredients that form the basis of many recipes. Other flavouring ingredients can be added, including chocolate, coffee, lemon juice and zest, and dried fruits. Each addition alters the basic cake flavour.

Sugar

Not only added for sweetness, sugars produce the structure and texture, so it is important to use the correct one:

Caster (superfine) sugar is available in white and unrefined golden varieties. It blends easily with fats when beaten or 'creamed' into light sponge mixtures.

Granulated sugar may be coarse white or golden and unrefined, and is used for toppings.

Demerara (raw) sugar is golden in colour and has a grainy texture. It is often used for recipes where sugar is melted over heat, or as a decorative crunchy topping.

Soft light and dark brown sugars cream well and usually form the base of a fruit cake, or are used in recipes where a rich flavour is required. Store them in an airtight container.

Muscovado (molasses) sugar is natural and unrefined, with a dark colour and rich flavour that makes fruit cakes and gingerbreads special.

Icing (confectioners') sugar is sold as a fine white powder or in an unrefined golden form. It is used for

BELOW: *clockwise from bottom left, Caster sugar, runny honey, granulated sugar, demerara sugar, soft light and dark brown sugar, black treacle, golden syrup, icing sugar, and muscovado sugar are all sweeteners with their own clearly defined flavours.*

ABOVE: *Eggs and buttermilk.*

icings, frostings and decorations. Store the sugar in a dry place, as it tends to absorb moisture. Sift the sugar at least once, or preferably twice, before you use it, as it may form hard lumps during storage.

Golden (light corn) syrup, honey, treacle and molasses are liquid sugars used in cakes that are made by the melting method.

Eggs

Although they are often stored in the refrigerator, better results will be achieved if eggs are kept at room temperature. The eggs whisk better, and will achieve more aeration. Aeration gives volume and allows the eggs to blend into mixtures easily. Cold eggs tend to curdle a mixture.

Medium-size eggs are used in the recipes in this book, unless otherwise stated in the recipe.

Dried egg-white powder gives good results and can be substituted in royal icing recipes, or in recipes where you are unsure about the suitability of using raw egg whites. Raw eggs are unsuitable for the elderly, pregnant women, babies and young children.

Flours

Plain (all-purpose) flour provides the structure of a cake but contains nothing to make it rise. Richer cakes that do not need raising agents are made with plain flour.

Self-raising (self-rising) flour has raising agents in it. These create air in the batter to make a cake rise, so it is used for sponges and light mixtures that contain little or no fruit. If you have only plain flour, add 12.5ml/2½ tsp baking powder to every 225g/8oz plain flour to make self-raising flour.

Wholemeal (whole-wheat) and brown flours contain bran from the wheat, which provides texture and fibre. This keeps cakes and breads moist and gives a mellow flavour. If you are substituting brown flour for white in a recipe, add extra liquid, as the bran will absorb more fluid.

White flours can be kept in a cool dry place for up to six months, but wholemeal flours will not keep for as long because they have a higher fat content. Check the use-by date on packs of all types of flour. Flour is best stored in an airtight container, which should be washed and dried before refilling. Don't add new flour to old, as small micro-organisms that look like tiny black specks may form, and will spread into new flour. Keep all flour dry, as damp flour weighs more and alters the measurements in a recipe, which could lead to failure.

ABOVE: *Clockwise from bottom left, Plain, strong, wholemeal, brown, and self-raising flours.*

Separating egg whites and yolks

When separating egg whites from their yolks, tip the whites into a cup one at a time so that if there are any specks of yolk or pieces of shell in the cup, you can remove these easily. If yolk is present in a bowl of whites it will inhibit whisking and aeration of the whites. Even a tiny speck of yolk will stop the whites from whisking up to a foam and you will have wasted the whole mixture.

Raising agents

These produce an airy and light texture. Small quantities are used, so they need to be measured accurately.

Baking powder is a mixture of bicarbonate of soda (baking soda) and cream of tartar. When liquid is added, the powder bubbles and produces carbon dioxide, which expands during baking and creates an airy texture.

Bicarbonate of soda (baking soda) is gentler and is used to give heavy melted mixtures a lift.

Cream of tartar is a fast-acting raising agent that works as soon as it touches liquid.

Buttermilk

When added to recipes that use bicarbonate of soda (baking soda), buttermilk acts as a raising agent.

The acidity mixed with bicarbonate of soda produces carbon dioxide, which raises the mixture as it cooks. Make your own souring agent by mixing 290ml/10fl oz low-fat yogurt or milk with 5ml/1 tbsp lemon juice.

Fats

As well as giving flavour and texture to cakes, fats improve keeping qualities. Butter gives the best flavour to cakes. Soft tub margarine is suitable only for all-in-one sponge recipes where all the ingredients are mixed in one bowl and need an extra raising agent. Don't overbeat recipes using soft tub margarine, as the mixture will become wet and the cake will sink. Do not substitute this fat for butter or block margarine as it will not produce the same results.

Vegetable shortenings are flavourless but can be used to produce very pale, light cakes.

Cooking oils can be used successfully in moist cakes such as carrot cake. As they do not hold air, the mixture cannot be creamed and these cakes have a dense texture.

Basic equipment

If you're new to baking, start off with some mixing bowls and utensils and a few pans. A 900g/2lb loaf tin, a 20cm/8in cake pan and a muffin tin are all useful.

Baking papers, paper cases and foil

For lining tins (pans) and baking sheets, use baking parchment, which is non-stick (waxed) paper. Paper cases come in sizes to fit round or square cake tins or cupcake and muffin tins. Waxed paper is a useful surface to pipe royal iced decorations on to, so they peel off easily once dry. Kitchen foil is good for wrapping rich fruit cakes or to protect wrapped cakes in the freezer.

Baking sheets

Choose large, heavy-duty baking sheets. Non-stick sheets are useful, but avoid thin bakeware, which might bend during baking.

BELOW: Paper cases can be purchased to fit an exact tin size, but you can make your own from sheets of baking parchment.

ABOVE: *Mixing bowls, wooden spoons, palette knives, flexible scrapers and a skewer or cake tester are basic equipment.*

Bowls

You'll need a set of different sizes of bowls for mixing and beating small and large amounts of cake batters, eggs, cream and other liquids.

Electric whisk

A hand-held electric whisk makes quick work of whisking cake batters and egg whites, and is an invaluable aid for cake-making.

Flexible scraper

A flexible scraper is perfect for getting the maximum amount of cake batter out of a bowl.

Grater

A grater with a fine and a coarse side is useful for grating citrus rinds, chocolate and marzipan.

Kitchen scales

Accurate kitchen scales are vital. Scales with a pan and weights are just as good as digital scales, as long as they are accurate.

ABOVE: *An electric mixer and whisk are helpful and time-saving kitchen tools, making light work of beating cake batters.*

Measuring spoons and cups

Use standard measuring spoons for small quantities of ingredients. Remember that all spoon measures should be level. Kitchen tablespoons or teaspoons may be inaccurate.

Metric and imperial are given in the recipes. Follow one set of measurements, as they are not exactly equivalent.

Graded measuring cups are used in many countries in place of kitchen scales and are handy for quick measuring. A measuring jug (cup) is vital for liquids and it needs to be graduated in small measures.

Oven

Always preheat the oven to the correct temperature before putting a cake in to bake. Before you switch on the oven, arrange the shelves so that the tins (pans) will fit.

Fan-assisted ovens circulate hot air around the oven and heat up quickly. If you are using a fan oven, reduce the temperature stated in the recipe by 10 per cent If the oven is too hot, the outside of a cake will burn before the inside cooks. If it is too cool, cakes may sink or not rise evenly. Do not open the oven door until halfway through the baking time, as a drop in temperature will stop the cake rising.

Palette knife or spatula

These are ideal for loosening cakes from their tins (pans), lifting cakes and smoothing on icing and frostings.

Pastry brush

A pastry brush is necessary to brush glazes over cakes and to brush melted butter into tins. A spare brush is useful as they wear out quickly.

Scissors

Use to cut lining papers and snipping dried fruits or nuts into chunks.

Sieves (Strainers)

A large wire sieve is used for flour and dry ingredients, and a small nylon sieve for icing (confectioners') sugar.

BELOW: *Useful kitchen equipment includes sieves, graters, scissors, pastry brush and a large palette knife.*

Skewer or cake tester

A thin metal skewer can be used to test if a cake is ready.

Spoons

Keep a large wooden spoon just for baking. Don't use one that has been used for frying onions, as the flavours may taint the cake batter. Use a metal spoon for folding flour and egg white into batter.

Tins (Pans)

Always use the size of tin stated. If you use too large a tin, your cake may be too shallow. Too small a tin may cause a peak to form, which will crack or sink in the middle.

Choose good-quality rigid bakeware, which will give better results. Non-stick coatings on bakeware need almost no greasing and cakes turn out well, as do cakes made in flexible muffin and loaf moulds.

Sandwich tins and shallow round tins will bake sponges quickly.

Loaf tins in small and large sizes are ideal for teabreads and loaf cakes.

BELOW: *Measuring jug, kitchen scales, measuring spoons and cups are essential for accurate baking.*

ABOVE: *A selection of tins (pans) in different sizes and shapes increases the range of baked goods you can make.*

Deep round and square heavy cake tins are ideal for baking fruit cakes.

Springform tins are round with a clipped side that can be loosened and removed easily from delicate bakes such as light sponges or cheesecakes. Muffin tins have 6 or 12 indentations with deep-set muffin holes for larger individual cakes.

Fairy cake, bun or patty tins are similar to muffin tins but have shallower indentations for making smaller cakes. Line each indentation with a paper case.

Ring moulds and Kugelhopf tins are round metal moulds with a hole or funnel in the centre, and are designed for baking angel cakes and ring-shaped cakes. Grease with melted butter, and put small strips of baking parchment in the base of plain ring moulds to aid the release of the cake.

Wire racks

These allow air to circulate around the hot baked cakes so that they cool without becoming moist underneath.

Successful cake-making

Paying attention to the detail of a recipe will help to ensure a perfect cake. First, get all your equipment ready and prepare your cake tin. Take care with accurate measuring, and know how to test that the cake is cooked so that your hard work is rewarded with a delicious treat.

Assembling the ingredients

Ensure that you have all the necessary ingredients ready before you start baking.

Sifting flour makes a fine-textured product that is light and airy.

Accurate weighing and measuring

Recipes usually specify imperial, metric or cup weight. For good results, you must follow one set only and never use a combination, as they are not exact equivalents. If the measurements are muddled, it will affect the quality of the baked goods.

1 All spoon measurements must be level using a recognized set of metric or imperial spoon measures. Never estimate weights, as you will rarely achieve an accurate result.

2 As ingredients must be measured exactly, use good kitchen scales for weighing or graded measuring cups and scoops. These cups should be levelled for accurate measuring unless the recipe calls for a 'generous' cup.

Preparing tins (pans)

When recipes give instructions on how to prepare and line tins, don't skip this, or you may ruin the baked cake. If using tins without a non-stick coating, give them a light greasing before use. Line the base of a tin to help the cake turn out easily.

1 Apply a thin film of melted butter with a pastry brush, or use kitchen paper and softened margarine.

Lining the sides of the tin

1 Cut a piece of baking parchment or greaseproof (waxed) paper 2.5cm/1in wider than the depth of the tin and long enough to fit around the circumference. Make a fold along one long edge of the strip, about 2.5cm/1in deep. Snip the edge at intervals with sharp scissors. Cut a round of paper to fit the base of the cake tin.

2 Line the sides of the tin using the strip, with the snipped edge at the base, lying flat. The baking parchment should adhere to the greased tin. Lightly grease any overlap of the edges so that it doesn't protrude into the cake batter, which would make the base of the cake uneven. Fit the round of paper to cover the snipped edge. If your tin has a loose base this will stop the batter from escaping and burning on the oven base.

Lining the base of a tin

1 With the tin on a sheet of baking parchment, draw around it. Cut out.

2 Fit the rounds of paper in the base of the tin to cover the snipped edge.

Additional lining

1 Fold baking parchment double and 5cm/2in higher than the tin sides then continue as for 'Lining the sides of the tin' (opposite). Wrap brown paper around to protect the cake.

Lining a baking tray

1 Cut paper larger than the tray. Snip into each corner, then press in place.

Coating with flour

1 Tip a spoonful of flour into the greased tin, then tip away the excess.

Filling a cake tin (pan) with batter

1 Spread cake batter evenly to the edges. Rub off any drips from the tin.

Checking to see if a cake is cooked

There are ways to determine whether a cake is ready. Has it baked for the suggested time? The baking times may need reviewing if you know that your oven temperature is inaccurate, if other items are being cooked at the same time, or if the oven door is opened in the baking process.

1 Cakes should be golden, risen and firm to the touch when pressed lightly in the centre. Lighter sponges and cakes should be a pale golden colour and the sides should shrink away from the sides of the tin (pan).

2 To test a cake, insert a thin skewer into the centre. If the cake is cooked, it should come out perfectly cleanly with no mixture sticking to it. If there is mixture on the skewer, bake the cake for a little longer and test again.

Different methods of making cakes

There are six basic ways to make cakes. Each method gives the cake a different texture and consistency. To get perfect results, it's important to know how the different types of mixture should be prepared.

Classic creaming method

Light cakes are made by the creaming method, in which butter and sugar are first beaten or 'creamed' together. A little care is needed to achieve a perfectly creamed mixture.

1 In a large bowl, with either an electric whisk or a wooden spoon, beat the fat and sugar together until pale and fluffy. As the sugar dissolves it blends with the fat, lightening it and making it very soft.

2 Add the eggs one by one, beating after each addition, to form a batter. Eggs are best used at room temperature to prevent the mixture from 'splitting' or curdling.

3 Adding a teaspoon of flour with each beaten egg will help to keep the mixture light and smooth and prevent the mixture from separating. A badly mixed and curdled batter will hold less air and be heavy, and can cause a sunken cake.

All-in-one method

This one-stage method is quick and easy, and it's perfect for those new to baking, as it does not involve any complicated techniques. It is an ideal method for making light sponges. Softened butter or tub margarine at room temperature must be used.

1 All the ingredients are placed in a large bowl and quickly beaten together for just a few minutes until smooth. Do not over-beat, as this will make the mixture too wet.

Rubbing-in method

This method is used for easy fruit cakes and small buns such as rock buns. In this method, the fat is lightly worked into the flour between cold fingers, in the same way as for making pastry. The fat should ideally be cold.

1 Rub the fat into the flour with your fingertips until the mixture resembles fine crumbs. This can be done by hand or using a food processor. Keep it cool and trap air in the mixture by lifting it up as you rub in the fat. Shake the bowl to allow the larger lumps of fat to rise to the surface, then rub in the larger lumps. Repeat the rubbing-in process until an even crumb is achieved.

2 Stir in enough liquid to give a soft mixture that will drop easily from a spoon.

Melting method

Cakes with a moist and sticky texture, such as gingerbread, are made by the melting method. These cakes use a high proportion of sugar and syrup and may contain heavier grains such as ground nuts or oats. They benefit from storing for at least a day before cutting.

1 Over a gentle heat and using a large pan, warm the fat, sugar and syrup, until the sugar has dissolved and the mixture is liquid. Stir now and then, but check that the sugar does not burn on the base of the pan.

2 Allow the mixture to cool a little then add the flour, eggs, spices and remaining ingredients to make a batter. Bicarbonate of soda (baking soda) is often used in this method, to help raise a heavy batter. These cakes rise but the texture is heavier.

Whisking method

Light and feathery sponges are made by the whisking method. These are not easy cakes for beginners. The only raising agent is the air trapped in the mixture during preparation. As the air in the mixture expands in the heat of the oven, the cake rises. Fatless sponges such as a Swiss roll (jelly roll) are made this way.

1 A classic sponge is made by whisking eggs and caster (superfine) sugar over a pan of hot water until the batter is thick enough to leave a trail when the whisk is lifted away from the bowl. When the mixture is pale, thick and airy, remove the bowl from the heat and continue to whisk until cool and doubled in volume.

2 Add the flour by sifting some over the surface and folding it in, using a large metal spoon, until evenly blended.

3 Be gentle; don't knock out the air bubbles when folding in the flour.

Making fruit cakes

Rich fruit cake recipes begin with the creaming method, then fruits and nuts are folded in with the flour.

1 Cream the butter and sugar in a large bowl, add the eggs, a little flour, and here, treacle (molasses).

2 Add the flour and any spices, then add the dried fruits last, stirring well to incorporate all the ingredients.

Fillings and toppings

Cakes are made extra special by adding a filling or topping, and there are many different coverings to suit a variety of uses. Use sugarpaste icing on celebration cakes, or frostings on gateaux, or decorate with simple frosted flowers.

Buttercream icing

This rich icing makes a good cake covering and filling, or can be used to stick sugarpaste icing to cakes. Flavourings such as citrus rind or coffee can be added.

Makes 350g/12oz/2 cups

75g/3oz/6 tbsp unsalted butter, softened
**225g/8oz/2 cups icing (confectioners')
    sugar, sifted**
5ml/1 tsp vanilla extract
10ml/2 tsp milk

1 Place the butter, icing sugar and vanilla extract in a bowl and whisk or beat with a wooden spoon.

2 Add the milk and beat until soft, smooth and fluffy. Store, chilled, for up to 2 days in a covered container.

Ganache

This rich icing, made from chocolate and cream, makes a perfect topping or filling for a rich chocolate cake for a special occasion.

Makes 350g/12oz/2 cups

250ml/8fl oz/1 cup double (heavy) cream
**225g/8oz plain (semisweet) chocolate,
    broken into pieces**

Gently heat the double cream and chocolate in a large, heavy pan, stirring until melted. Pour into a bowl, leave to cool, then spread over the cake.

Vanilla frosting

Use this smooth and creamy frosting as a filling and topping.

Makes 150g/5oz/scant 1 cup
**150g/5oz/generous 1 cup icing
    (confectioners') sugar**
25ml/5 tsp vegetable oil
15ml/1 tbsp milk
**a few drops of vanilla extract or a little
    vanilla bean paste**

Sift the icing sugar into a bowl and beat in the oil, milk and vanilla extract or vanilla bean paste until smooth and creamy.

Chocolate fudge frosting

Rich and tasty, this glossy frosting can be poured over a cake or used to spread inside a cake as a filling, or to cover the cake as a topping.

Makes 350g/12oz/2 cups

**115g/4oz plain (semisweet) chocolate,
    broken into pieces**
50g/2oz/½ cup unsalted butter
1 egg, beaten
**175g/6oz/1½ cups icing (confectioners')
    sugar, sifted**
2.5ml/½ tsp vanilla extract

1 Melt the chocolate and butter in a bowl set over a pan of gently simmering water.

2 Remove from the heat and whisk in the egg, icing sugar and vanilla. Whisk until the frosting is smooth. Use at once or leave to cool and thicken.

Glacé icing

This icing can be used to drizzle over sponge cakes.

Makes 225g/8oz/1½ cups

225g/8oz/2 cups icing (confectioners') sugar
a few drops of vanilla extract
30–45ml/2–3 tbsp hot water
food colouring (optional)

1 Sift the icing sugar into a bowl and add flavouring. Gradually add enough water to mix to a consistency of thick cream.

2 Beat with a wooden spoon until the icing is thick enough to coat the back of the spoon. Add colouring, if you like, and use at once, as the icing will begin to form a skin. Liquid food colourings are ideal.

Glacé icing Variations
• Citrus: Replace the water with freshly squeezed, strained orange or lemon juice.
• Chocolate: Sift 10ml/2 tsp unsweetened cocoa powder into the icing (confectioners') sugar.
• Coffee: Dissolve 5ml/1 tsp coffee granules in 15ml/1 tbsp of hot water, then cool, or add 5ml/1 tsp liquid coffee extract.

Making a paper piping (pastry) bag

Paper piping bags are useful for piping with or without a nozzle.

1 Cut out a 38 × 25cm/15 × 10in rectangle of baking parchment. Fold it diagonally in half to form two triangles. Cut along the fold line.

2 The long edge of the triangle forms the top opening edge of the piping bag. Roll one short side of the triangle into the centre to make a sharp-pointed cone, and hold in place at the centre. Fold the other end around the cone.

3 Hold the points at the back of the cone. Keep the pointed end sharp. Fold the outer layer inside the top edge to hold in place. Keep the layers together. Snip a tiny hole at the tip. Part-fill with icing. Fold over the top.

Crystallized decorations

Flowers, berries, petals and leaves can all be crystallized and make a perfect addition to special cakes.

1 Wash herb sprigs, leaves or edible berries, then pat dry with kitchen paper. Leave to dry.

2 Separate petals from rosebuds, and brush small flowers such as violets or primroses using a clean paintbrush, but do not wash them.

3 Beat 1 egg white with 15ml/1 tbsp cold water until frothy.

4 Liberally paint the herbs, leaves, berries or petals with egg white.

5 Sprinkle with caster (superfine) sugar while damp, shake off any excess. Dry on waxed paper in a warm place. Attach to the cake with royal icing.

Apricot glaze

Use for sticking almond paste to a cake or to add a shiny finish to toppings.

Makes 450g/1lb/2 cups

450g/1lb/1 cup apricot jam
5ml/1 tsp lemon juice

1 Heat in a pan with 45ml/3 tbsp water. Boil fast for 1 minute.

2 Press through a fine sieve (strainer).

3 Pour into a clean jar and store in the refrigerator for up to 3 months.

Almond paste

Marzipan seals the cake and makes a flat area for icing.

Makes 450g/1lb/2 cups

115g/4oz/1 cup sifted icing (confectioners') sugar
115g/4oz/generous ½ cup caster (superfine) sugar
225g/8oz/2 cups ground almonds
1 egg
5ml/1 tsp lemon juice
15ml/1 tbsp brandy

1 In a bowl, mix the sugars and ground almonds together.

2 Whisk the egg, lemon juice and brandy. Mix into the dry ingredients.

3 Knead the almond paste until smooth. Wrap in clear film (plastic wrap) and store in the refrigerator for a maximum of 3 days.

To use almond paste

1 Knead on a surface lightly dusted with icing (confectioners') sugar until soft. If the paste has been chilled, bring it to room temperature first.

2 Place the cake upside down on a cake board so that the top is level. Measure the circumference of the cake using a piece of string.

3 Brush the cake all over with apricot glaze. Fill in the gaps around the base with a rope of almond paste. Fill any holes or dips with pieces of paste.

4 Evenly roll out the almond paste to a square or circle large enough to cover the top of the cake. Cut out the circle or square, then press it on top of the cake.

5 Roll a sausage of almond paste the length of the string, then use a rolling pin to roll it deep enough to cover the sides of the cake. Trim the edges. Roll it into a coil.

6 Roll the coiled strip around the side of the cake and press it on with the palms of your hands. Trim if necessary, and leave to dry out for at least 24 hours.

Royal icing

Use royal icing to cover Christmas or wedding cakes.

Makes 500g/1¼lb

2 medium egg whites
500g/1¼lb/5 cups icing (confectioners')
  sugar, sifted
10ml/2 tsp lemon juice

1 Put the egg whites into a clean, grease-free bowl and whisk with a fork to break up the whites until foamy.

2 Sift in half the icing sugar with the lemon juice, and beat well for 10 minutes, or until smooth.

3 Gradually sift in the remaining icing sugar and beat again until thick, smooth and brilliant white. Alternatively, use a hand-held electric mixer set on a slow speed to make the mixing easier.

4 Keep the royal icing covered with a damp cloth until you are ready to use it, or store in the refrigerator in a tightly lidded plastic container until needed. If making royal icing ahead of time for use later, beat it again before use to expel any air bubbles that may have formed in the mixture.

5 To cover a cake, spread the icing over the top and sides of the cake using a palette knife or metal spatula, then smooth down over the sides or flick into points with a knife to make a snowy effect. Leave the icing to dry and become firm for 3 days.

Cook's Tip

For a softer royal icing that will not set too hard, beat 5ml/1 tsp of glycerine into the mixture. Glycerine is sold bottled in liquid form in pharmacies and larger supermarkets.

Sugarpaste icing

This soft icing is also sold as roll-out icing, ready-to-roll icing or fondant icing. If you are covering a large cake or a tiered cake, make the sugarpaste in batches. It is suitable for covering a Madeira cake, or a fruit cake that has first been covered in almond paste.

Makes 350g/12oz/2 cups

1 egg white
15ml/1 tbsp liquid glucose
350g/12oz/3 cups icing (confectioners')
  sugar, sifted, plus extra for dusting
paste food colouring, if required

1 Mix the egg white and liquid glucose in a mixing bowl and stir with a fork, breaking up the egg white. Add icing sugar gradually, mixing in with a flat-bladed knife until the mixture forms a ball.

2 Turn out on to a clean surface dusted with icing sugar and knead for 5 minutes, or until soft but firm enough to roll out. If it is too soft, knead in a little more icing sugar.

Colouring sugarpaste

1 Colour the paste gradually and knead well to colour evenly.

Index